Welcome to the Screaming Chicken Cafe: MSM-Minimalialist Murmurings of a Meandering Mind

Collected Poems
Volume 1

"The Screaming Chicken"
Kyra Mulvany
(CY 2018)

BLUE SKY. BLUE SEA. FEEL-
ING BLUE, I SING THE BLUES: LIFE'S
VIEWS TINTED BY BLUE HUES.
(1996)

Welcome to the Screaming Chicken Cafe: MSM—Minimalialist Murmurings of a Meandering Mind

Collected Poems
Volume 1

KALEN PRESS LLC

MICHAEL SHANE MULVANY

Imprint: Kalen Press, LLC
Dover, DE 19901

Christopher J. O'Shea V, Publisher
Email: coshea00@gmail.com

ISBN: 978-1-7368062-3-4 [Print]
978-1-7368062-4-1 [MOBI]
978-1-7368062-5-8 [ePub]

Interior design by Booknook.biz

Cover design by Shelley Savoy

DEDICATION

FOR MY CHILDREN:
KYRA, MCKENNA, AND STUART

MY MIND SEES WHAT MY
SOUL FEELS. MY HEART SINGS THESE, MY
REALITIES. ME.
(2088)

KAILUA KONA, HI
JANUARY 10, 2022

TABLE OF CONTENTS

POEMS

PREFACE

MULVANY, O'SHEA
BID YOU *BIEN VENUE!* EN-
JOY THE SCREAM'S MENU.
(2114)

INTRODUCTION

"Welcome to the Screaming Chicken Café: MSM–Minimalist Murmurings of a Meandering Mind"- Collected Poems, Volume I, by Michael Shane Mulvany, is an initial compilation of more than 2,000 verses composed in the traditional Japanese senryu poetry form.

Senryu poems, like its haiku cousins, are structured in three lines, alternately featuring 5/7/5 syllables per line. While the two styles of composition are closely related, senryu poems tend to impart observations about intrinsically human foibles, whereas haiku poems tend to be about nature and the physical world. Senryu are often mischievous and darkly humorous in content, whilst haiku are ostensibly more 'serious' in their meaning and intent.

Each poem is assigned a unique number enclosed in parentheses. Numbers assigned reflect the order in which a particular poem was composed from first to last. Within each thematic section, poetic verses are presented in their reverse order of composition in order to permit the reader to readily trace the evolution of the author's creative musings over time.

Christopher J. O'Shea V, Editor
Kailua Kona, HI
March 27, 2022

BOOK ONE

ABOUT LIFE

OVERTHINKING, LIKE
DRINKING, DULLS OUR INSTINCTS,
DRIVES EMOTIONS EXTINCT.
(2111)

SWEATING SMALL STUFF MAKES
LIFE TOUGH. MACRO'S DO-ABLE;
MICRO'S RUE-ABLE.
(2109)

LIFE'S A ONE AND DONE.
EXTEND YOUR PLAY'S RUN: SEEK OUT
EACH DAY'S RAYS. FIND FUN!
(2108)

ALLOWING OTHERS
TO DEFINE YOU, LET'S THEM DESIGN
YOU – CONSIGN YOUR VIEWS.
(2103)

MOST CONSTRUE YOUR SI-
LENCE AS TACIT COMPLIANCE.
IF NOT TRUE, SHOUT OUT!
(2101)

DON'T LET THE WORST BURST
HOPE'S BUBBLE. REFLECT. REBOUND.
REBUILD FROM RUBBLE.
(2097)

PRAISE IS OVER-RATED.
LET MONEY DO YOUR TALKING.
MUCH APPRECIATED.
(2090)

I'LL LOOK YOU STRAIGHT IN
THE EYES, TELL YOU WHAT I THINK:
NO GAMES, GUILE, LIES.
(2085)

PURPOSE IS OFTEN
CONFUSED WITH REASON: ONE'S YOUR
WHY; ONE'S, ITS EXCUSE.
(2084)

REGRETS? MANY. DO
I CARE? WELL ...SPRING'S IN THE AIR;
ALL'S FAIR; SAVOIR FAIRE!
(2064)

TIME, WE LET SLIP A-
WAY IS LIFE'S RENT, SPENT IN PLAY.
BUDGET IT EACH DAY.
(2063)

WE CAN'T KNOW WHAT WE
DON'T KNOW, SAVE THAT IT'S MUCH MORE
THAN WHAT WE DO KNOW.
(2057)

LIFE'S LESSONS, SPURNED BY
YOUTH'S DIGRESSIONS, BURN IN WITH
AGEING'S CONFESSIONS.
(2056)

CONTEMPT'S A CONCEIT
OF EGO'S RETREAT INTO
SELF: PSYCHIC DECEIT.
(2049)

FOR MANY REAL-
ITY'S HARD, FANTASY EA-
SY: IT SETS THEM FREE.
(2048)

CLARITY IS A
RARITY, UNTIL WE AD-
MIT *"I'M FULL OF S@&T."*
(2046)

PERSPECTIVE DEPENDS
ON ONE'S EXPERIENCES. KEEP
THAT IN PERSPECTIVE.
(2036)

THERE'S NO SUCH THING AS
IDÉE FIXE: LIFE'S A MUTA-
TING BAG OF TRIED TRICKS.
(2034)

TERRIFIED SOMEONE
MIGHT GET *"IN"*, WE WEAVE SELF PRO-
TECTIVE WEBS, THEN *"SPIN."*
(2032)

LIMITING YOUR POINTS
OF VIEW RESTRICTS YOU MORE THAN
ANY JAIL WOULD DO.
(2030)

LIFE'S MESSY. WE ALL
HAVE CLEANING TO DO ...GET IT
DONE BEFORE YOU'RE THROUGH.
(2024)

DESTINY DEMANDS
HER DUE: NOW OR THEN. ONLY
SHE CAN SEE HOW – WHEN.
(2021)

ENABLERS SAY THEY'RE
DOING FAVORS WHILE SETTING
YOU UP FOR FAILURES.
(2016)

IN THOSE DARK HOURS WHEN
DOUBTS SPROUT, BLOOMING FLOWERS OF
PENDING GLOOM, WAKE UP!
(2013)

ON THE MAZE THAT'S MAN'S
SOCIETIES, A HAZE OF
HATRED SHROUDS THEIR WAYS.
(2011)

WHEN YOUR BACK'S TO THE
WALL, NOTHIN' TO LOSE, FIND THE
GALL TO MAKE *THEM* CHOOSE.
(2009)

MOST DON'T KNOW THEY'RE LED
AROUND BY THE NOSE. THEY SWEAR
IT'S JUST HOW LIFE GOES.
(2008)

YOU'VE GOT TWO CHOICES
IN LIFE: RIDE IT OUT OR PACK
IT IN. CHOOSE. BEGIN.
(2006)

BIRTH: IT'S ADMISSION
PRICE BUYS YOU GUILT, ANGER, SUF-
FERING AND – WAIT: DEATH.
(2005)

FEELINGS AREN'T MEANINGS.
THEY'RE POSSIBILITIES: HOP-
INGS, SCHEMINGS, DREAMINGS.
(2003)

EVIL ABIDES IN
MAN'S DNA; HIDING, GUID-
ING, LEADING ASTRAY.
(2000)

ACCEPTING MEDI-
OCRITY, AS YOUR DUE, WILL
DEBILITATE YOU!
(1993)

FREEDOM'S NOT A RIGHT.
IT'S NOT WON WITHOUT A FIGHT
OR KEPT WITHOUT MIGHT.
(1989)

PASS THROUGH. THAT'S ALL WE
DO. CAN'T CHOOSE THE TIMES. ACCEPT,
MAKE IT WORK FOR YOU.
(1988)

STARE IN A MIRROR.
WHO DO YOU SEE? YOU – TRUE – OR
THE YOU YOU'VE BECOME?
(1986)

SEEKING FAIR? IT'S NOT
THERE. SO -- GOT TO MAKE IT UN-
FAIR, IN YOUR FAVOR.
(1970)

APPREHENSION AND
TENSION ARE LIFE'S BORN WITH PEN-
SION: THEY FUND OLD AGE.
(1969)

IN MAN'S HISTORY
THEIR SOCIAL *"WE"* HAS HAD ONE
ROLE: TOTAL CONTROL.
(1968)

IN TIMES OF PLENTY
MOST BOAST, *"ME!"* *"ME!"* WHEN THINGS LOOK
BLEAK, THEY BLEAT, *"WE!"* *"WE!"*
(1967)

ANTICIPATE! IT
WILL HAPPEN. WAIT! MIGHT CATCH YOU
NAPPIN'. ... YOUR PAST'LL BITE.
(1960)

KNOW WHAT YOU CAN, WITH-
IN REASON, CONTROL. THE REST'S
EGO. JUST LET GO.
(1958)

FEW THINGS ARE INEV-
ITABLE; PROBABILILI-
TY BIRTHS CERTAINTY.
(1947)

TIME LOST – AH! DEAR COST! –
CANNOT BE REGAINED. CHERISH
THAT WHICH YOU'VE RETAINED.
(1945)

MAN'S WAYS, DIVERSE, ARE
BLESSING AND CURSE: EMBRACING
AS THEY'RE CHANGE AVERSE.
(1941)

SOME EASILY MAKE
MONEY, BUT CANNOT KEEP CLOSE
FRIENDS OR FAMILY.
(1940)

ALL OUR FRAILTIES MAY
BE OVERCOME, SAVE THIS: SELF
DECEIT IS RUIN'S KISS.
(1937)

THINGS WE DO STICK WITH
INVISIBLE GLUE: NO TIME
LIMITS – PAYBACK'S DUE.
(1934)

YOU SEE WHAT YOU WANT
TO SEE. I DO, TOO. THEN WE
ALL DENY THAT'S TRUE.
(1933)

TEMPIS FUGIT; CAN'T
UNDO IT; TOO SOON RUE IT;
WE MISCONSTRUE IT.
(1928)

TRYING A LITTLE
GETS YOU A LOT. NOT TRYING
A LOT GETS LITTLE.
(1927)

OBLIGATIONS, MOST
SELF-IMPOSED, FORCE YOU TO FO-
CUS ON THOSE – NOT YOU.
(1925)

LIFE'S A DEAL YOU MAKE
WITH YOU: STEADY, SEE IT THROUGH,
OR GIVE FATE ITS DUE.
(1924)

IN A LEAVING THERE
IS A BEGINNING. LOSING
CAN BECOME WINNING.
(1922)

HUMBLY, I SUGGEST
MORE HUMILITY, LESS
HOSTILITY, IS BEST.
(1917)

SIGH NOT FOR WHAT MIGHT
BE. CRY NOT FOR WHAT SHOULD BE.
TRY FOR WHAT CAN BE.
(1915)

MY FREEDOM CAN'T BE
AT YOUR EXPENSE. ALL OR NONE.
THE REST IS NON-SENSE.
(1914)

INTELLIGENCE IN-
FORMS DECISIONS. EGO DIC-
TATES THEIR PRECISION.
(1912)

THERE'S NO CERTAINTY
IN LIFE. WE CAN'T GUARANTEE
ANYTHING WILL BE.
(1905)

I'VE FLOWN THE HEIGHTS, DIVED
THE DEPTHS, NEVER QUITE CATCHNG
MY BREATH. THAT'S LIFE ... RIGHT?
(1903)

LET'S SEE: WHAT'S CHANGED SINCE
BUDDHA, JESUS, MOHAMMED
TAUGHT? ... TECHNOLOGY.
(1901)

THE TRUTH ABOUT TELL-
ING THE TRUTH IS: FEW CAN TELL
WHO'S TELLING THE TRUTH.
(1894)

WHEN NEAR IS FAR AND
CLOSE DISTANT, YOU GOTTA MOVE
ON NOW, THIS INSTANT!
(1886)

WHAT'S LEFT UNSAID OUGHT
NOT TO BE. THAT LEAVES FILL-IN-
BLANKS AND MAYBES.
(1883)

IN A RUT? THINK ON
TUT. HAD IT ALL; DIED AT NINE-
TEEN. FATE MAKES ITS CALL.
(1880)

MOST CHOICES DEFER
TO *"EASIER."* THESE END UP
MAKING LIFE HARDER.
(1879)

"ASK NOT – OWE NOT" OUGHT
TO BE TAUGHT TO ALL. FAVORS
SOUGHT, PUT US ON CALL.
(1878)

WHEN WRONG IS DONE, PRESS-
URE MOUNTS TO SETTLE ACCOUNTS.
BEEN THERE. IT'S NOT FUN.
(1871)

TRED LIGHTLY. DANCE THROUGH
LIFE SPRITELY. GRIN AT AFFLIC-
TION – MAN'S CONNECTION.
(1870)

PROSPERITY IS
RARELY LINKED TO TIMERI-
TY. LIVE, LOVE, BOLDLY.
(1869)

LISTEN WITH ONE EAR
TO WHAT PEOPLE SAY. WATCH WITH
BOTH EYES WHAT THEY DO.
(1868)

CONFIDENCE LOST EX-
ACTS SOUL-SAPPING COSTS: ANGER;
HEARTACHE; SURRENDER.
(1866)

LIFE CAN BE MESSY.
BUT THOSE CLEAN-UPS IN BETWEEN
GIVE US LUSTROUS SHEEN.
(1863)

PSYCH 101: YOUR
CALAMITY MIGHT BE MY
OPPORTUNITY.
(1860)

WHY'S ARE ELUSIVE,
EXCLUSIVE TO EACH ONE'S U-
NIQUENESS ... SO DON'T ASK!
(1855)

PROPRIETY'S AN
INEXACT NOTION: WHAT OF-
FENDS YOU MIGHT CHARM ME.
(1851)

IF WE DON'T AGREE
MOST DEPLORE US. SO MUCH FOR
"DO UNTO OTHERS ..."
(1841)

WE'RE ALL CONFUSED BY
SOCIETY'S RUSE – THE MYTH
THAT WE'RE FREE TO CHOOSE.
(1838)

NEVER UNDERES-
TIMATE THE CORROSIVE AR-
TISTRY OF EGO.
(1837)

ALL LIFE SHARES, INSTINCT-
IVELY, ITS ONE – AND ONLY –
RULE: WIN AT ALL COSTS!
(1828)

EACH LIFE IS VIEWED OUT
OF FOCUS. NO ONE CAN KNOW
OUR WHYS EXCEPT US.
(1827)

SEEKING PERFECTION'S
LIKE ATTAINING RESURREC-
TION – ONLY HARDER.
(1826)

PEACE OF MIND'S ELUS-
IVE. SAY YOU FIND IT: NOTHING'S
CONCLUSIVE ... DON'T QUIT.
(1823)

IT'S NOT IF SOMEONE
WILL TRY TO *"GET EVEN."* BUT
WHEN. THEY'RE *"JUST HUMAN!"*
(1820)

WE PRETTY MUCH KNOW
WHEN IT'S TIME TO GO, THEN E-
GO WAILS *"I CAN'T FAIL."*
(1819)

MOST TAKE PASSION AS
NEUROTIC EMOTION OR
CHILDISH COMMOTION.
(1813)

INTENTIONS ARE LIKE
TO-DO LISTS TOSSED IN A DRAWER:
THEY'LL GET DONE ... PROMISE!
(1809)

TRUE RESPECT SHOULD NEV-
ER BE EXPECTED. YOU HAVE TO
LEARN IT TO EARN IT.
(1805)

THERE'S WORSE THINGS THAN NOT
PLAYING FAIR – LIKE RIGGING THE
GAME -- SO FAIR'S NOT THERE.
(1793)

REFS IN ALL SPORTS WILL
ATTEST PLAYERS AND FANS SWEAR
THEY KNOW MORE – AND BEST!
(1791)

CONSUMATION BRINGS
ELATION: NOT AS MUCH AS
ANTICIPATION.
(1788)

AIN'T NOTHING FREE. THERE'S
ALWAYS A PAYMENT DUE. SOME-
TIMES MONEY. MOST TIMES YOU.
(1784)

TRUTH'S SUBJECTIVE; MEM-
ORY'S SELECTIVE. SEE WHY
NO ONE'S OBJECTIVE?
(1780)

THINK SOMETHING'S NEW IN
THE DOINGS OF MEN? NOT TRUE.
RECYCLED – AGAIN.
(1778)

IT MATTERS NOT HOW
WE POSTURE AND PRETEND. ALL
KNOW HOW THIS WILL END
(1777)

WE'RE ALL EQUAL – SOME
MORE SO (WE JUST KNOW!). THE REST
MUST BE KEPT IN TOW.
(1776)

CONTRITION DOESN'T COME
FROM WINNING. LOSING IS IT'S
CRUCIAL BEGINNING.
(1772)

HOWL IN THE WIND! DEEP
BREATH, THEN DO IT AGAIN. LET
A NEW YOU BEGIN!
(1771)

HISTORY, REPLETE
WITH VICTOR'S STRICTURES, DOESN'T REN-
DER COMPLETE PICTURES.
(1769)

HABIT SNEAKS UP LIKE
A SNAKE – UNSEEN – THEN ITS GRIP
IS TOO FIRM TO BREAK.
(1767)

DON'T GET INVOLVED WITH
POLITICS. WE HAVEN'T EVOLVED
MUCH THERE SINCE ROCKS/STICKS.
(1765)

INEQUITY IN
CAPACITY FOR EMPA-
THY ALLOWS *ME! ME!"*
(1763)

THE CAUSE OF OUR DE-
MISE ISN'T A SURPRISE: EGO,
DECEIT AND THEIR LIES.
(1762)

WE SHARE THIS LIFE WITH
MANY. FEW, IF ANY, SEE
IT THE WAY WE DO.
(1761)

IT MATTERS WHERE WE
GO, BUT HOW WE GET THERE SHOWS
IF, AND WHEN, WE'LL GROW.
(1760)

CONSEQUENCES HAVE
NO SEQUENCES: NOW. THEN. LA-
TER. YOU WON'T KNOW WHEN.
(1759)

LOOSE THAT SHACKLED *'ME'*.
LET YOUR SOUL, UNFETTERED, FLY
HIGH, SOARING LIGHTLY.
(1754)

LIFE'S LESSONS: NEVER
QUIT; DON'T MAKE A BIG DEAL OF
IT; KEEP MOVING ON.
(1753)

INTERELATED, BUT
SEPARATED, OUR MIND OR HEART
CAN RIP US APART.
(1750)

LIFE'S FULL OF POSSI-
BILITIES AND RIFE WITH COULD-
A, SHOULDA, MAYBES.
(1749)

WORDS UTTERED IN HASTE
OR DESPAIR WILL FIND A WAY
TO BITE YOU *"DOWN THERE."*
(1748)

ASK NOT WHY YOU'RE HERE,
RATHER, *"WHAT CAN I DO TO
FILL MY LIFE WITH CHEER."*
(1744)

THE EFFORT REQUIRED
TO KNOW WHAT YOU DON'T KNOW IS
INSPIRED, NOT ACQUIRED.
(1742)

THE BEST OF US ARE
FEW. THE REST OF US DEPEND
ON ALL THAT THEY DO.
(1741)

SEE? IT ALL COMES DOWN
TO *"AM I READY"* -- FOR WHAT-
EVER? GOTTA BE.
(1740)

CLARITY IS NOT
VERITY. WE CAN *"SEE"* CON-
CEPTS AND NOT *"KNOW"* THEM.
(1739)

TOO BAD LIFE'S NOT A
BALANCE SHEET. MOST CAN'T MAKE THEIR
CREDITS - DEBITS MEET.
(1738)

REALITY IS
NOT TOTALITY. BE O-
PEN TO FANTASY.
(1736)

MENTAL AGILI-
TY DOESN'T GUARANTEE PERSON-
AL STABILITY.
(1735)

I'VE BEEN THE ONE WHO
WON. I'VE BEEN LAST. WINNING'S FUN.
LOSING TEACHES FAST.
(1734)

I DON'T KNOW A LOT
SAVE THIS: LIFE DOES NOT OWE YOU
A HUG AND A KISS.
(1730)

NOT MUCH MATTERS. THEN
WE'RE GONE. LIFE GOES ON: STARS LIGHT
NIGHT, SUN SHINES AT DAWN.
(1729)

MOST TIMES WE DO WHAT
WE HAVE TO. A FEW TIMES WE
DO WHAT WE WANT TO.
(1728)

MORALITY IS
LEARNED – AND LOST – BY EXAMPLE.
WHAT'RE OUR TIMES' SAMPLES?
(1727)

MOST EXISTENCE IS
AT THE WHIMSY OF QUITE FLIM-
SY SOCIAL PRETENSE.
(1725)

BEING OPEN MINDED
AIN'T EASY. MOST ARE BLINDED BY
EGO'S CREDO: *"ME"*.
(1724)

TOO MANY BORROW
FROM TOMORROW THEN PRAY IT'LL
GET THEM THROUGH TODAY.
(1723)

MODESTY IMPELS
TO MODERATION. VANI-
TY BREAKS THAT SPELL.
(1714)

WORDS LEFT UNSPOKEN
OFTEN CAUSE HEARTS – AND LIVES – TO
BE BROKEN. SAY THEM!
(1708)

WHEN WE WERE NEW, I
DIDN'T KNOW WHAT TO DO. OLDER,
BOLDER, I ASK YOU.
(1707)

THERE'S MORE *'OUT'* THAN *'IN'*.
THERE'S MORE *'HAS BEENS'* THAN THOSE WHO
WIN. HOW YOU DOIN'?
(1705)

RUDE NEED NOT BE LEWD
OR CRUDE, JUST PRESENT A HINT
OF LATENT CONTEMPT.
(1697)

I DON'T INTUIT
OR THINK THROUGH IT. WHAT I DO
IS, SIMPLY, DO IT.
(1696)

LIFE – THE HIGHEST STAKES
GAME. WINNER TAKES ALL. LOSERS
FALL. IN? OUT? YOUR CALL.
(1694)

WITH ALL LIFE'S BUSTLE
AND FUSS, WE RARELY SEE HOW
FAST TIME HUSTLES US.
(1684)

DON'T ADVISE; DON'T SELF-
ADVERTISE; ONLY TELL WHITE
LIES; SEEK COMPROMISE.
(1683)

THERE'S TWO WAYS TO VIEW
NEWS THESE DAYS: GOSPEL OR
PROPAGANDA. SHOW TIME!
(1682)

WANTING INCLUSION
BRINGS ANXIETY AND CON-
FUSION. BE YOU – FREE.
(1680)

THERE'S NO WINNING WITH-
OUT LOSING. WE'VE GOT TO LEARN
HOW TO WIN. 'TIL THEN …?
(1676)

TENACITY CAN'T
BE ACQUIRED: IT'S A PRODUCT
OF HOW ONE'S HARD WIRED.
(1675)

PURVEYORS OF DE-
CEIT, USE IGNORANCE'S CON-
CEIT TO DEFEAT TRUTH.
(1674)

ESCHEW RELIGION
AS PHILOSOPHY. IT'S PER-
SONAL ... YOURS ONLY.
(1672)

SOME REFLECTION'S NEEDED.
TOO MUCH FREEZES YOUR MIND, LEAVES
DANGER SIGNS UNHEEDED.
(1671)

BEING: EXISTEN-
TIAL; DOING: POTENTIAL; LIVING:
SHORT TERM RENTAL.
(1669)

IGNORANCE BIRTHS PRIDE,
VANITY. NOT QUITE INSAN-
ITY. CLOSE, BUT WIDE.
(1668)

SUPPOSITION'S OF-
TEN BRING *"BACK AGAINST THE WALL"*
POSITIONS. ASK FIRST.
(1665)

A FREEWAY TO NO-
WHERE'S MORE OFTEN CHOSEN THAN
THE TRAIL TO *"I'M THERE."*
(1664)

ASKED WHY THEY DO WHAT
THEY DO MOST REPLY: *"DON'T KNOW,
NEVER THOUGHT IT THROUGH."*
(1663)

SOME DO. SOME DREAM THEIR
WAY THROUGH LIFE (BEST TO AVOID
COMMITMENT AND STRIFE).
(1662)

YOUNG: I PRAYED I'D LEAVE
SOMETHING TO PASS ON. AGED: NO
ONE WILL CARE I'M GONE.
(1661)

ONLY ONE THING'S CER-
TAIN: UNCERTAINTY. THE REST?
POSSIBILITY.
(1660)

YOUR HEAD SHOULD BALANCE
YOUR HEART, NEVER LEAD, TO GIVE
YOUR LIFE IT'S BEST CHANCE.
(1659)

TEMPIS FUGIT. WE
ABUSE IT 'TIL IT'S ABOUT
RUN OUT – THEN RUE IT.
(1656)

POGO SAID IT LONG
AGO: *"WE'VE MET THE ENE-
MY AND HE -- IS US!"*
(1654)

INTROVERSION IS AN
AVERSION TO LIMELIGHT. EX-
TROVERTS MUST SHINE BRIGHT.
(1652)

WE ALL LIKE TO FEEL
LIFE IS OUR CALL. TRUTH: MOST ARE
THEIR OWN WRECKING BALL.
(1651)

TIME'S A UNIQUE GAME.
FOR ANY TWO IT DOESN'T PASS
THE SAME. WHAT A SHAME.
(1648)

ENSNARED IN LIFE'S RIFTS
AND VALLEYS, FEW REVEL IN
ITS GIFTS – THEN RARELY.
(1646)

WHEN YOUR LIGHT SHINES FROM
WITHIN, THEN LIFE, ALWAYS A
FIGHT, IS A SURE WIN.
(1645)

THE ABYSS 'TWIXT WHAT
WE NEED AND WHAT WE WANT IS,
SIMPLIFIED, THIS: GREED.
(1644)

ANTICIPATION
STIMULATES. ITS ACTUAL-
IZATION DEFLATES.
(1643)

STOPPING TO SMELL THOSE
ROSES, PRESUPPOSES ONE
CAN AFFORD TO DWELL.
(1642)

SOME RUN THROUGH LIFE. SOME
CRAWL. A FEW DANCE. THEY GET IT:
TAKE A CHANCE. YOUR CALL.
(1641)

WHINING *"WHY ME?"* HEAR
YE: LIFE DISCRIMINATES IN-
DISCRIMINATELY.
(1639)

INTUITION CAN'T
BE TAUGHT, LEARNED OR BOUGHT. A THING
FEELS RIGHT OR – IT'S NOT.
(1626)

FEELING STUCK? CHEER UP!
RECALL LIFE'S ONE CONDITION –
CHAOS RUN AMOK!
(1625)

JURY'S OUT. IT'LL NEV-
ER COME IN. WITHOUT A DOUBT,
MAN'S GUILTY AS SIN.
(1624)

SHOULD'VE LET MY HEART RULE.
INSTEAD, I CAVED-IN TO MY
HEAD. SIMPLE, WRETCHED FOOL.
(1623)

TO BELIEVE IN GOOD'S
NAÏVE. TO HOPE? FINISH THIS:
"GIVEN ENOUGH ROPE ..."
(1622)

MOST LIVE BY THE CON.
REASONS VARY: EGO, FUN.
FAME, MONEY – GAME ON!
(1621)

THE ONE'S WHO CHOOSE TO
OBEY RULES ARE THOSE WITH SOME-
THING TO LOSE AND FOOLS.
(1620)

MOST DIE ERE THEY LIVE,
THEIR SPIRIT NOT EQUAL TO
THAT WHICH LIFE DOTH GIVE.
(1619)

TRUST GOD AND SAM COLT.
GIVE REMINGTON A NOD. THUS,
ENDETH THE LESSON.
(1618)

PLAYING IT STRAIGHT AND
NARROW MAKES IT EASY FOR
FICKLE FATE'S ARROW.
(1617)

MOST WILL BE NICE, IF
IT MEETS THEIR PRICE. ... SEE HOW THEY'LL
BE IF IT'S FOR FREE.
(1615)

HAS THERE BEEN A TIME
WHEN POLITICS WASN'T A LI-
CENSE TO COMMIT CRIMES?
(1614)

I HAVE EMPATHY
FOR YOUR MISERY. BEEN THERE.
... BUT NO SYMPATHY.
(1609)

FACE IT PLAIN AND SQUARE:
AIN'T NOTHIN' ABOUT LIFE THAT'S
FAIR. GO GRAB YOUR SHARE.
(1608)

MOST DAYS THE WAYS OF
MEN ARE THOSE OF SIN. NOW AND
THEN, LOVE SNEAKS A WIN.
(1606)

WHEN DREAMS COME TRUE, FEW
KNOW WHAT TO DO. DREAMIN'
AIN'T DOIN'! BOO HOO!
(1605)

I'M CONVINCED. THERE'S TOO
LITTLE EVIDENCE, PROVING
MAN HAS ANY SENSE!
(1602)

TO BE A PLAYER,
YOU HAVE TO BE A PAYER.
NOTHING'S FREE. GOLLY!
(1598)

MOST CHOOSE TO CONFUSE
THEIR LIVES WITH LIES, THEN ALI-
BIS. DON'T ASK THEM WHY.
(1597)

THOSE WHO DO IT KNOW
YOU GOT TO LEAN INTO IT
TO GET THROUGH IT … LIFE.
(1596)

TRY TO FORGIVE – ONE
CAN'T LIVE FULLY WITH REGRET –
YET … NEVER FORGET.
(1595)

OUR TALE OF WOE IS
SNEAKY, YOU KNOW. SIMPLY TOLD,
WE GET TOO SOON OLD.
(1594)

NAÏVE, YOUTH BELIEVE
TRUTH'S FIXED. THEY CAN'T YET SEE IT'S
SUPPLE PLIANCY.
(1593)

FATE'S LIKE ROULETTE: MAKE
A CHOICE, SPIN THAT WHEEL. REGRET?
REJOICE? LOSE? WIN? CHOOSE.
(1592)

IN TIMES OF PLENTY,
NOT MANY THINK ABOUT WHEN
PLENTY WILL RUN OUT.
(1591)

PURPOSE IS PERSON-
AL. RARELY RATIONAL, MOST-
LY EMOTIONAL.
(1589)

FEW HESITATE TO
HATE. INFUSED FROM BIRTH, THEY CAN'T
WAIT TO VINDICATE.
(1588)

OVER, UNDER, UP,
DOWN, AROUND AND THROUGH. THAT'S LIFE.
DO WHAT YOU CAN DO.
(1583)

A TIMELY PAUSE WILL
OFTEN CAUSE CLARITY TO
SHINE BRIGHTLY. GO SLOW.
(1581)

WEEP, NOT LEAST, FOR EM-
PATHY'S DEATH. CARING'S CEASED,
BARING MAN AS BEAST.
(1579)

YOU FEW WHO TAKE LIFE
SERIOUSLY SEE, POIGNANT-
LY, IT'S GIFT ISN'T FREE.
(1576)

AFTER WANTIN' AND
GETTIN' COMES HAUNTIN' AND
REGRETTIN'. WHICH IS WORSE?
(1571)

WHEN BOLD-FACED LIES FAIL,
ACCESSORIZE WITH TEARY
EYES AND MOURNFUL WAILS.
(1569)

MOST DON'T WANT TO KNOW,
WHAT THEY DON'T KNOW – MAKES THEM VUL-
NERABLE, FEEL LOW.
(1568)

LEARNING THE HARD WAY'S
A SLOW, PAINFUL ART, BUT WHEN
YOU EARN SMARTS THEY STAY.
(1563)

KNOW THIS! MOST PEOPLE AREN'T
REALISTS. THEY ARE RE-
MORSELESS SOLIPSISTS.
(1562)

CONTROL'S AN ILLU-
SION FOR THOSE TOO SCARED TO FACE
LIFE'S CONFUSION. YOU?
(1553)

SOME PATHS WE CHOOSE ARE
ONE WAY. WITH FEW CLUES, IT'S RARE
NOT TO GO ASTRAY.
(1550)

STRATEGIC LIES SHOULDN'T
BE A SURPRISE ... YOU WON'T LOOK BAD
AND THEY WON'T GET MAD.
(1544)

MOST SAY, *"YOU'VE GONE A-*
STRAY." THEY CAN'T CONCEIVE WE'D CHOOSE
TO DO THINGS OUR WAY.
(1541)

LIFE AIN'T TOUCH-
Y FEELY, TWO HEART'S BEATIN'. C'MON! IT'S
EAT -- OR BE EATEN.
(1540)

CONSTANT YEARNING KEEPS
MY BRAIN CHURNING WITHOUT CEASE.
ONLY YOU BRING PEACE.
(1539)

WE'RE ALL BORN TO BE,
AS WE TOO SOON SEE, ALONE.
THUS, LIFE'S IRONY.
(1538)

RELIEF'S A BELIEF
ALL'S WELL. MAN'S TIME HAS THIS TO
TELL: IT'LL NEVER BE.
(1537)

I'LL STAY. WE'LL PLAY. BUT …
YOU BETTER NOT BETRAY TRUST
OR, SOMEHOW, YOU'LL PAY.
(1536)

CHOICES NOT THOUGHT THROUGH
OFTEN LEAD TO LIFE-TIME IS-
SUES, DREAMS NOT COME TRUE.
(1535)

EGO'S *"ME"*- CENTERED
POWER, ALLOWED FREE REIGN, WILL
DEVOUER EMPATHY.
(1533)

RUMINATION'S BEEN
THE RUINATION OF MAN-
Y – INCLUDING ME.
(1530)

O.K. EVERY-
ONE, IN UNISON, SAY *"I
WILL LISTEN TODAY!"*
(1527)

SOMETIMES WE HAVE LOTS.
SOMETIMES NOT. DEPENDS ON HOW
MUCH MONEY WE GOTS.
(1526)

WE WANT WHAT WE WANT,
NEED WHAT WE NEED. IF IT'S RIGHT
OR NOT – FEW PAY HEED.
(1525)

IF YOU JUST SEE THE
FINISH LINE, YOU'LL MISS ALL THE BEAU-
TY IN A DESIGN.
(1524)

EGALITARI-
AN: A TERM ONLY USED BY
PROLITARIANS.
(1523)

LIFE COMES DOWN TO THESE:
LOVE, FAMILY, CAREER. WISH
IT DID SO WITH EASE.
(1521)

C'MON! JUMP IN. TAKE LIFE
FOR A SPIN. CAN'T WIN. GOT NOTH-
IN' TO LOSE. LET'S CRUISE.
(1519)

THE GOODNESS OF TOO
FEW TEMPTS ONE TO DOWNGRADE THE
EVIL MOST MEN DO.
(1518)

AN ATTACHMENT TO
HUMANITY ASSURES LOSS
OF ONE'S SANITY.
(1516)

YOUR ATTITUDE'S RUDE,
CRUDE AND NEEDS TO BE DISCON-
UED. SO, SCRAM, DUDE!
(1515)

WHEN YOU HAVE EVER-
Y THING, BUT DON'T HAVE YOURSELF,
THEN YOU HAVE NOTHING.
(1514)

WHAT YOU GIVE TO LIFE
MIGHT NOT BE GIVEN BACK TO
YOU. THAT SHOULDN'T STOP YOU.
(1513)

TOO FEW ARE INSTINCT-
IVELY HONEST. MOST SEEK TO
MISCONSTRUE – AT BEST.
(1512)

GOODNESS ISN'T INHER-
ENT, BUT LEARNED. ITS FRAGILE MER-
CIES MUST BE DISCERNED.
(1510)

WHEN THE BEAUTY OF
TWINKLING STARS AND A FULL MOON
DOESN'T MAKE YOU SWOON – HOWL!
(1504)

LIFE'S COURSE GETS DAMMED AND
DIVERTED. GO WITH ITS FLOW, WHILE
STAYING TRUE TO YOU.
(1502)

IF YOUR TRUTH ISN'T MINE,
FINE. LET'S AGREE ON A LINE
WITH SHARED BOUNDARIES.
(1501)

LIFE'S NO BOARD GAME TO
WIN OR LOSE. IT'S A SCAVEN-
GER HUNT WITH FEW CLUES.
(1489)

IN IT, OF IT, TRY-
ING TO RISE ABOVE IT: STILL-
I YEARN TO LOVE LIFE.
(1488)

MY PREDILECTION
FOR TRUTH HAS THIS AFFLICTION:
MOST PREFER FICTION.
(1487)

IT'S NOT WHAT WE SAY,
BUT THE WAY: TONE, INFLECTION
MAKE THE CONNECTION.
(1477)

BEING YOURSELF FOR
EACH PERSON CAN'T BE DONE … ON-
LY WITH THE RIGHT ONE.
(1473)

MOST WON'T HEAR BOTH SIDES
OF AN ARGUMENT: IT BRINGS
FEAR AND DISCONTENT.
(1471)

SOMETIMES THE *"RIGHT THING"*
ISN'T RIGHT. MAYBE THE *"WRONG THING"*
MIGHT BE. WAIT … LEARN … SEE.
(1469)

SILENCE: UNDERRATED,
RARELY ANTICIPATED.
TO BE HEARD, *LISTEN*.
(1458)

THE MORE ONE IS O-
PEN, THE LESS THEY'LL BE COPIN' –
WITH LOTS LESS MOPIN'.
(1454)

LIFE PLAYS ITS HAND CLOSE
TO THE CHEST. BEST NOT BLUFF … THE
COMPETITION'S ROUGH.
(1453)

VALIDATION IS
SECOND BEST TO CONSUMA-
TION: PURE ELATION.
(1451)

YOU THINK TIME'S YOUR FRIEND?
C'MON! EACH SECOND THAT TICK-TOCKS
YOU'RE CLOSER TO GONE.
(1448)

THE WORLD, AND NO ONE,
OWES YOU A THING. IF THIS IS
NEWS, YOU'VE LEARNED NOTHING.
(1446)

YOU LAUGH, CRY, SING, DANCE,
BUT DON'T BELIEVE IN RISKING
A CHANCE. WHO'S SUFFERING?
(1441)

THE TIMES IN LIFE WE'RE
FREE FROM STRIFE ARE, REGRETA-
BLY, NOT THAT MANY.
(1434)

THE DEPTH OF MOST SELF-
DECEPTION DETERS DETEC-
TION. WE DIVE HEAD FIRST.
(1433)

MOST AREN'T WHO THEY SEEM
TO BE. WE PROJECT OUR I-
DEAL REALITY.
(1431)

MOST OF LIFE COMES DOWN
TO BUCKS. YOU GOT'EM, YOU WIN.
IF NOT … THEN IT SUCKS!
(1427)

TRUST, A MUST IN ALL
THAT WE DO, IS MOST CRUCIAL
BETWEEN YOU AND – YOU!
(1404)

THE TRULY WISE (FEW)
ESCHEW JUDGMENT. DISCOURSE – PRO
AND CON – SERVES IN LIEU.
(1388)

A CAPACITY
TO WITHSTAND FATE'S BOTTOM-DEALT
HAND UPS THE ANTE.
(1387)

THE HURRY-WORRY
OF URBANITY IS, AT
BEST, INSANITY.
(1380)

THOSE TOLLING BELLS WON'T
CEASE THEIR KNELLS, 'TIL MANKIND FINDS
A SHARED PIECE OF MIND.
(1375)

YOU SAY YOU'RE RIGHT. I
SAY MY LEFT'S YOUR RIGHT. WHO'S RIGHT?
WHAT'S LEFT TO SAY, RIGHT?
(1374)

IT'S NOT WHAT YOU KNOW
SO MUCH AS WHAT THEY THINK YOU
KNOW. GO FOR THE SHOW.
(1371)

PREDICTABLE IS
VULNERABLE. SO – BEST TO
BE VARIABLE.
(1370)

PLAYING THE *"WHAT-IF?"*
GAME'S A SHOO-IN BALLET TO
LOSERS HALL OF FAME.
(1366)

PERFECTION'S A SCHEM-
ERS PROJECTION; AN IDYLL
DREAMER'S CONFECTION.
(1363)

PURPOSE IS SUBJECT-
IVE. JUST AS ALL DEFINI-
TIONS ARE ELECTIVE.
(1361)

WANTING DOESN'T GET. WEEP-
ING FORFEITS ACTION: TO NO-
ONE'S SATISFACTION.
(1360)

SELL YOUR SOUL FOR WHAT-
EVER SUM AND YOU'LL REGRET
IT 'TIL KINGDOM COME.
(1358)

A FANTASY OF
AGONY AS ECSTACY
IS SHEER LUNACY.
(1354)

NOTHING'S FAIR OR FREE.
BOTTOM LINE? MONEY. ALL THE
REST IS JUST SHOW BIZ.
(1352)

AIN'T MUCH WE CAN DO
ABOUT MOST THINGS 'CEPT WAIT 'TIL
THE FAT LADY SINGS.
(1351)

I'M FED UP WITH FEAR
AND ANXIETY. FEED ME
BEER AND GAITY.
(1349)

YOU DON'T SEE ME
LIKE I SEE ME. LET'S AGREE: YOU'LL
BE YOU, I'LL BE ME!
(1346)

THE PATHS TO HELL ARE
MANY. MOST DON'T NEED ANY.
THEY FIND THEIR OWN WAY.
(1344)

NEVER UNDERES-
TIMATE IGNORANCE. DON'T AS-
SUME INTELLIGENCE.
(1341)

THOSE WHO REFUSE TO
LEARN FROM THEIR MISTAKES, RISK IG-
NORANCE AND HEARTACHE.
(1339)

O.K. BECAUSE I
KNOW WHAT TO DO, DOESN'T MEAN I
KNOW HOW TO DO IT.
(1335)

FEEL LIKE SCREAMING? DO
THIS: LEARN TO BE DEVIOUS
AND SCHEMING. PURE BLISS!
(1332)

THERE'LL SOON COME A DAY,
WHEN WE ALL HAVE TO PAY FOR
WHAT WE DO – AND SAY.
(1328)

THE YOU *YOU* WANT TO
BE MIGHT NOT BE THE YOU *YOU*
NEED TO BE. TOUGH CALL.
(1320)

A SELECTIVE MEM-
ORY FREES ONE FROM ALL RE-
SPONSIBILITY.
(1319)

SOCIETY IS
EMPATHY. WHEN THAT ATRO-
PHIES, WHERE WILL WE BE?
(1318)

WHEN YOU GO ALL IN
YET, STILL, DON'T WIN, TOUGH UP, DUST
OFF, THEN TRY AGAIN.
(1315)

WISHING MOTIVATES.
PLANNING ACTIVATES. WORK GEN-
ERATES. GET GOING!
(1314)

WHAT WOULD BE THE GREAT-
EST SIN? EASY. THE MOTHER
OF THEM ALL: ENVY.
(1311)

WE WIN, OR LOSE, BY
WHAT WE CHOOSE, OR REFUSE, TO
DO. IT'S UP TO YOU.
(1305)

YOU FEW WITH INSIGHTS
TO CREATE, CAN'T KNOW WHAT EN-
VY THEY GENERATE.
(1304)

HOW MUCH IS ENOUGH?
WHAT'S GOOD? OR BAD? YOU TELL ME.
I DOUBT WE'LL AGREE.
(1294)

EACH DAWN LIGHTS HOPE'S RE-
BIRTH. EACH SUNSET SHADES BODIES
INTERRED IN SCORCHED EARTH.
(1293)

I DECLINE TO O-
PINE ON TOPICS DIVERSE TO
SILENCE THOSE AVERSE.
(1291)

THE DELICACY
OF VANITY OFT TILTS TO-
WARD INSANITY.
(1288)

DON'T CLING TO WHAT'S GONE
TOO LONG. MAKE IT PART OF YOUR
HEART'S SONG, THEN MOVE ON.
(1280)

RISK AVERSE, I A-
VOID *"FOR BETTER OR WORSE."* I'LL
STICK WITH *"SAFETY FIRST."*
(1279)

THERE'S NO DEATH MORE MOURNED
THAN TRUTH SET TO FIRE. BY THESE
FLAMES DOES LIGHT EXPIRE.
(1277)

DON'T CREEP OUT THE BACK
DOOR. IF YOU'RE GONNA GO, DO
SO, WITH A LOUD ROAR!
(1259)

HERE'S A CLUE FOR WHAT
NOT TO DO: NEVER ASSUME
YOU KNOW WHAT TO DO.
(1258)

IT'S EASY TO MIS-
CONSTRUE WHAT OTHERS DO WHEN
YOUR FOCUS IS ON YOU.
(1250)

ANGER'S RUSH TO RAGE
WON'T BE CONTROLLED IF ITS OWN-
ERS CAN'T BE CONSOLED.
(1249)

CAN'T BE WHAT YOU'RE NOT.
TAKE YOUR BEST SHOT, THEN BE CON-
TENT WITH WHAT YOU'VE GOT.
(1248)

TICK-TOCK. WATCH TIME RACE
AROUND THE CLOCK FACE. IT WON'T
SLOW FOR YOU. TICK-TOCK.
(1235)

PROBABILITY
INDICATES. SENSIBILI-
TY DELINEATES.
(1229)

THAT WHICH COMES AT GREAT
COST CAN BE TURNED FROM A THING
LOST TO A THING LEARNED.
(1228)

CAUTION'S GREAT – AS LONG
AS IT DOESN'T PREVENT ONE FROM
DOING WHAT *"RIGHT"* DICTATES.
(1227)

VERY FEW OWN UP
TO WHO THEY KNOW THEMSELVES TO
BE ... CAN'T ... TOO SCARY.
(1226)

BEST TO LEAVE A CRACK
IN DOORS YOU CLOSE. MIGHT NEED TO
OPEN ONE OF THOSE.
(1222)

HISTORY BEING
"PASSÉ", MAN HAS TO RE-LEARN
WHAT WORKS – THE HARD WAY.
(1216)

NO ONE CAN FORCE YOU
TO QUESTION YOUR SOUL. ONLY
YOU CAN TAKE THAT POLL.
(1211)

COMPROMISE IS THE
BALM OF LIFE. WITHOUT IT THERE'S
NOUGHT BUT ENDLESS STRIFE.
(1210)

ROGUE-ISH CHARM CAN'T HARM,
RIGHT? CAREFUL WHO YOU PLAY: MIGHT
BITE BACK HARD ONE DAY.
(1209)

THE WAY TO WIN IS
PRETEND TO LOSE, THEN GAIN YOUR
ENDS BY SUBTERFUGE.
(1208)

ALL'S FAIR. ANYTHING'S
IN PLAY. NOT MANY WILL CARE.
THE WORLD WORKS THIS WAY.
(1204)

FUN'S DONE. SERIOUS
HAS BEGUN. GOT TO MAKE IT
BEFORE TIME TAKES IT.
(1196)

PEOPLE ARE PEOPLE.
SOME ARE POISON, SOME SWEET. DON'T
LIMIT WHO YOU MIGHT MEET.
(1193)

I SLEEP. I DREAM. I
WAKE. I WORK. I COME HOME. I
SLEEP – I DREAM … MY LIFE.
(1190)

MOST ASPIRE TO LIVES
MUCH HIGHER. SWEET DREAMS FADE FAST
WHEN BILLS COME DUE.
(1189)

THAT CHILL CALM YOU FEEL
SERVES ONLY TO CONCEAL THE
FEAR YOU CLAIM ISN'T REAL.
(1187)

LOVE'S A LURE. IT LULLS
YOU INTO FEELING SECURE …
CAN'T EVER BE SURE.
(1184)

LIFE'S MOSTLY IN BE-
TWEENS. HIGHS AND LOWS COME AND GO –
LIVING'S IN THE SEAMS.
(1182)

THE UPSIDE OF DOWN
IS THAT ONCE YOU'RE DOWN, THERE'S NO
WAY TO GO BUT UP.
(1181)

THERE'S NO *"MAYBE"* TWIXT
ME AND THEE. SO, EITHER *"YES"*
OR I GO ON *"NO."*
(1180)

WE PLAY LIKE WE LIVE.
PLAY FAIR, YOU CARE. PLAY CHEAT, YOU,
YOUR LIFE, ALL DECEIT.
(1175)

LIFE'S NOT FAIR. VERY
FEW CARE. COMPASSION'S RARE. IT'S
DANGEROUS OUT THERE!
(1170)

HARD IS EASY. EA-
SY ISN'T. GOT TO WORK HARD
TO MAKE IT LOOK EASY.
(1162)

WE PLAY TO WIN. ALL
ELSE IS SPIN. GOT TO BE TOP
GUN. LOSING'S A SIN.
(1149)

ACCEPTING WHO YOU
ARE IS THE MOST DIFFICULT
PART OF LIFE – BY FAR.
(1146)

AN EXPRESS TRAIN! THAT'S
YOU: NO WAITIN', NO DEBAIT-
IN', JUST BARREL THROUGH.
(1143)

TRANSCENDING MORTAL-
ITY REQUIRES EMBRACING
ONE'S HUMANITY.
(1141)

TURN YOUR CHEEK, APPEAR
WEAK. BETTER TO BE PERCEIVED
AS STRONG – RIGHT OR WRONG.
(1136)

THERE ARE LIMITS ONE'S
NOT SUPPOSED TO EXCEED. BUT,
ALSO, NEED – AND GREED.
(1134)

THE DO AND DON'T OF
LOVE IS SIMPLE: WHAT SHE WANTS
"DO"; WHAT SHE DON'T *"DON'T."*
(1133)

COURTESY FLED WHEN
COMPROMISE DIED. ALL THAT'S
LEFT IS TO PICK A SIDE.
(1129)

TRYING TO BE SOME-
THING WE'RE NOT, WE GET CAUGHT UP
IN DECEIT'S CONCEITS.
(1128)

MINE'S NOT A STORY-
LINE TO INSPIRE. MORE LIKE A
NIGHTMARE, SET TO FIRE.
(1127)

AS MUCH AS MOST TRY
FOR *"WE'RE ALL ONE,* IT TURNS IN-
TO: *"ME" -- "MYSELF" -- "I."*
(1125)

EASY'S NEVER BEST.
WITHOUT LIFE'S LESSONS LEARNED, WE
WILL FAIL EVERY TEST.
(1123)

"THE TRUTH, THE WHOLE TRUTH,
AND NOTHING BUT THE TRUTH": TOLD
BY THOSE WHO WIN WARS.
(1121)

"BE GOOD, FOLLOWING
RULES", BOUGHT ME A BOW SEAT ON
MANKIND'S SHIP OF FOOLS.
(1119)

I DON'T POST, OR LIKE,
OR FOLLOW. DEVICE FREE, GUESS
THAT MAKES ME FALLOW.
(1118)

IT'S NOT ENOUGH TO
KNOW A THING. YOU HAVE TO SHOW
A THING TO BE TRUE.
(1116)

WHEN SLUMMING, APPEAR
TO BE BUMMING: SO SLICK,
SO CHIQUE, SO DEBONAIR!
(1115)

IF YOU AIN'T GONNA
'GO ALL IN', BETTER CASH OUT
AND NEVER BEGIN.
(1114)

TRACE AMOUNTS OF AF-
FECTION ARE NO DEFLECTION
AGAINST DEFECTION.
(1112)

UNFORESEEN, CAUGHT UP
IN ROUTINES, MOST SOON BECOME
ROBOTIC MACHINES.
(1111)

RANDOM THOUGHT: IF ONE
GOT ALL THEY WANTED – ENOUGH? … SURE
THOUGHT: FOR MOST FOLKS – NOT.
(1110)

THINKING'S FREE. SPEAKING?
JUST LET'S SAY, IT'S QUITE LIKELY
YOU WILL HAVE TO PAY.
(1109)

I'VE A HOPE OF HOPE.
IT'S LIGHT FLICKERING, I CAN'T
LET DOUBT SNUFF IT OUT.
(1108)

CHOICES DEFINE US.
THEY DESIGN OUR FATE. THINK TWICE,
AND THEN – HESITATE.
(1106)

WHERE DOES FINAL TRUTH
RESIDE? THAT, MY FRIENDS, IS WHAT
YOU HAVE TO DECIDE.
(1105)

PLANNING, HARD WORK YIELD
ACCESS TO SUCCESS – UNLESS
YOU'RE A LUCKY JERK!
(1104)

DON'T GET TOO SMUG OR
CUTE. WHAT YOU HAVEN'T DONE, COULD REN-
DER ALL YOU'VE DONE, MOOT.
(1103)

HIDING – HOLDING BACK –
WON'T GET YOU ON TRACK. TO KNOW
YOU GOTTA SHOW UP.
(1102)

ONLY FOOLS TRUST IN
HUMAN KINDNESS. WISE MEN
BANK ON MORAL BLINDNESS.
(1100)

THIS AIN'T NEWS: BAD THINGS
HAPPEN. WE FORGET. THEY HAP-
PEN AGAIN. NO SH-T!
(1098)

DON'T CEASE LAMENTING
THOSE WHO LOVED AND LOST. FEW WOULD'VE,
IF THEY KNEW THE COST.
(1097)

WE PLAY AT BEING
O.K. EVEN WHEN WE KNOW
IT'S RARELY THAT WAY.
(1094)

CAN'T BE WHO WE AIN'T.
MOST TRY – BLIND TO THE IRO-
NY IN THE CONSTRAINT.
(1086)

THE MORE WE KNOW, DOUBTS
GROW: COMPREHENSION STIMU-
LATES APPREHENSION.
(1085)

WHEN ASKED MY VIRTUES
TO EXTOL, I ROLL MY EYES,
SMILE, THEN SIGH, *"QUELLE DRÔLE!"*
(1084)

PLANT ME WHERE I FALL,
BOOTS AND ALL. IT AIN'T LIKE THERE'S
SOMEONE YOU SHOULD CALL.
(1083)

COMPASSION'S RARE. TO
HAVE IT, ONE MUST NOT ONLY
CARE, BUT ALSO SHARE.
(1079)

LIFE'S NEVER BEEN NICE
OR NEAT. GOTTA WIN EACH DAY
OR WIND-UP LUNCH MEAT.
(1078)

WISDOM DOESN'T SHOUT, *"I'M
HERE!"* SMALL INSIGHTS OVER TIME
DISPLACE DOUBT AND FEAR.
(1075)

WE DIDN'T CHOOSE TO EN-
TER THIS WORLD, BUT WE CAN DE-
CIDE HOW LIFE UNFURLS.
(1074)

NO ILLUSIONS MEANS
FEW CONCLUSIONS. WHEN I GO
NO ONE'LL CARE – OR KNOW.
(1073)

BEEN TRYIN' ALL THESE
MANY YEARS TO OVERCOME
MY FEARS. CLOSE. SO NEAR.
(1072)

MOST LIVES AREN'T THE ONES
WE'D CHOOSE, BUT ARE THE RESULT
OF ALL OUR CHOICES.
(1071)

PROSTITUTION'S NOT
THE OLDEST GIG. THEY MI-
MIC POLITICIANS.
(1055)

LIFE'S NOT NEAT, SMOOTH, FINE-
TUNED. IT'S THE CALM, GLASSY SEA
BETWEEN THOSE TYPHOONS.
(1050)

WANTS DELAYED INCREASE
TENSION, WHICH LEAVES NERVES FRAYED,
FRAUGHT WITH APREHENSION.
(1044)

"OLD, WIZZENED, *PASSÉ*,
WHAT COULD THEY KNOW", SAY TODAY'S
YOUTH "ABOUT OUR AGED TRUTH."
(1043)

LACKING MORAL COM-
PASS, EGO SWAGGERS, HEEDLESS,
INTO THE ABYSS.
(1042)

BEAUTY CAN CAST MA-
LEVOLENT SPELLS. IN IT'S GUISE,
EVIL OFTEN DWELLS.
(1036)

THE HEIGHT OF FOLLY
MOST SURELY IS ASSUMING
ABSENT INQUIRY.
(1031)

WHEN WE CHOOSE, WE MAKE
DEALS WITH OUR SOUL. TACIT, BIND-
ING, THERE'S NO APPEALS.
(1027)

SOME LEARN EASY, SOME
HARD. SOME DON'T LEARN – THESE LIFE HOISTS
ON THEIR OWN PETARD.
(1025)

PLEASE PROMISE YOU'VE READ
THE FINE PRINT. YOU KNOW, THAT PART
WHICH SAYS, *"I WON'T SPRINT."*
(1023)

STUCK IN NEUTRAL? OR,
EVEN WORSE, REVERSE? INSPIRE
YOURSELF, LOSE THAT CURSE.
(1022)

TO WIN'S NOT A VIC-
TORY. IT'S AFFIRMATION OF
ONE'S ABILITY.
(1020)

MOST OF US DON'T KNOW
OURSELVES WELL ENOUGH TO KNOW
WE DON'T KNOW OURSELVES.
(1012)

SO MANY THINGS WE
FAIL TO DISCERN, WHEN WE'RE TOO
SELF-ABSORBED TO LEARN.
(1011)

WE'RE ALL CREATURES AND
VICTIMS OF OUR PASSIONS. PRAY
WE LEARN SOME LESSONS.
(1004)

RIGHT AND WRONG: SHORT VER-
ION OR LONG? SHORT – DON'T GET CAUGHT.
THEN NOTHING IS WRONG.
(1003)

DO ALL YOU CAN TO
KEEP YOUR FLAME LIT. YOU GIVE UP
ON YOU WHEN YOU QUIT.
(997)

LIFE FAVORS THOSE WHO
IGNORE THE RULES. MOST PEOPLE
TAKE TO RECKLESS FOOLS.
(996)

O.K. LISTEN UP.
QUICK! GO! HAVE FUN. MASS EXTINCT-
ION SIX HAS BEGUN.
(993)

SOMETIMES THE LIFE YOU
PLANNED MAKES OTHER PLANS FOR YOU.
HANG IN THERE. STAY TRUE.
(991)

WE TRY TO KEEP OUR
WORD, DO GOOD. BUT, AT TIMES, WE
CAN'T DO WHAT WE SHOULD.
(989)

AT LEAST ONCE SOMEONE
WILL USE YOU FOR GAIN, THEN LOSE
YOU, LEAVE YOU IN PAIN.
(988)

WE'RE CONSUMED BY PRIDE;
EGOS THAT WON'T BE DENIED;
MOST KINDNESS HAS DIED.
(985)

MONEY'S NOT THE BEST
MEASURE OF WEALTH. THAT'D BE: LOVE,
RESPECT AND GOOD HEALTH.
(984)

RESPECT MUST BE EARNED.
IF YOU THINK OTHERWISE THERE'S
MUCH YOU HAVE NOT LEARNED.
(983)

'ROUND AND 'ROUND WE GO,
REPEATING THE PAST. WE RE-
LEARN FAST – IT DON'T LAST!
(982)

"IT'S FATE": WHAT IS SAID
TO RATIONALIZE SOMETHING
WE CAN'T COMPREHEND.
(980)

ONCE LOST, INNOCENCE
CAN'T BE RECLAIMED. THE HEART SOURS,
YOUR SOUL'S MAIMED. DARK FLOWERS.
(978)

NONE OF US ARE WHAT
WE PROJECT. THERE'S SO MANY
SECRETS TO PROTECT.
(977)

KINDNESS MAY INFLAME:
IF YOU RAISE HOPES AND THEY'RE NOT
MET, WHO GETS THE BLAME?
(976)

SPRING LOADED TO THE *"UP
YOURS"* POSITION LEAVES NO LEE-
WAY FOR CONTRITION.
(975)

SOME STUMBLE, RISE, MOVE
ON. OTHERS, AFRAID, ALONE, CAN'T
GET UP, TOO FAR GONE.
(968)

SEEMS LIKE YOUR DREAMS DIE
OF OLD AGE? WONDER WHY? YOU'RE
STUCK – TURN THE PAGE!
(962)

PRAY GOD YOU NEVER
CROSS A SOCIOPATH. THEIR'S
IS AN ENDLESS WRATH.
(959)

YOUR EGO'S BASED ON
LIKES AND TRENDING. THINK ABOUT WHAT
MESSAGE THAT'S SENDING.
(954)

SAY PLEASE, SAY THANK YOU.
ALWAYS BE HUMBLE AND KIND.
GIVE OTHERS THEIR CUE.
(953)

SILLY FOOLS, WE, JUDG-
ING BY APPEARANCES, IG-
NORING QUALITY.
(952)

MANY A LONG NIGHT
SPENT IN WHINY SELF-PITY
EARNED THIS INSIGHT: HELP!
(947)

ONE LIFE'S NOUGHT BUT A
GRAIN IN THE SANDS OF TIME – HERE;
GONE; FORGOTTEN... I'M!
(946)

WINNING AT ALL COSTS –
GOING FOR THE JUGULAR:
NOTHING'S UGLIER.
(945)

WHEN YOU HAVE TO DE-
BATE LONG IF SOMETHING'S RIGHT OR
WRONG; TOO LATE! ALL WRONG.
(944)

THE KEYS TO LIFE? LUCK
AND TIMING. WITHOUT EITHER
YOU'RE MOUNTAIN CLIMBING.
(943)

WHAT IS AND WHAT SHOULD
BE ARE SEEN DIFFERENTLY
BY YOU THAN BY ME!
(939)

IT TAKES HOW LONG IT
TAKES. SOME THINGS FAST, OTHERS SLOW.
THAT'S THE WAY WE GO.
(938)

YOUTH: COCKY, IMPUL-
SIVE; MIDDLE AGE: RIGHTEOUS, CER-
TAIN; OLD: W.T.F.?
(934)

TIME'S NOT YOUR FRIEND. DO
IT! DON'T DELAY. OUR END'S IN
SIGHT FROM THE FIRST DAY.
(927)

BE WHAT MAY, WE'LL ALL
HAVE A DAY WHEN DEBTS ARE DUE.
HOW'LL THAT PLAY FOR YOU?
(922)

THE MOST PERFECT THING
ABOUT A LOVE STORY IS
ITS IMPERFECTION.
(919)

THINKING THINGS THROUGH ISN'T
OVER-THINKING. BE THOROUGH,
CLEAR; NOT OBSESSIVE.
(915)

LEARN FROM YOUR PAST. MAKE
PLANS FOR A FUTURE, ALWAYS
LIVE IN THE PRESENT.
(914)

THERE'S TWO THINGS WE ALL
NEED TO KNOW: WHEN TO SAY YES
AND WHEN TO SAY NO.
(912)

MOST PEOPLE DON'T LIS-
TEN TO WHAT YOU SAY, AS MUCH
AS, HOW YOU SAY IT.
(908)

WE NEED DREAMS. PURSUE
THEM. JUST DON'T LET THEM GET IN
THE WAY OF LIVING.
(906)

TO THOSE WHOSE WORLD ENDS
AT THE TIP OF THEIR NOSE: YOU
WILL KNOW MANY WOES.
(892)

MOST IMBUE THE AGED
WITH CHILD-LIKE STATUS. THOSE OF
YOU WHO DO – UP YOURS!
(889)

TWO SINS DO US IN:
HYPOCRISY: I'M BETTER;
VANITY: I'M BEST.
(880)

SOLITUDE IS AN
ATTITUDE. MANY ARE A-
LONE IN A LARGE CROWD.
(876)

WE LURE OURSELVES WHO
RAPTLY STARE IN MIRRORS CON-
JURING WHAT ISN'T THERE.
(868)

WE'RE SO BLINDED BY OUR
PERCEPTIONS WE WON'T SEE BE-
YOND THEM: RIGHT OR WRONG.
(866)

MOST, CONFUSED, REFUSE
TO SEE THOSE SHADOWED FEW WHO
RUSE AND ABUSE THEM.
(863)

NURTURING RARELY
REAPS WHAT IT SOWS. NATURE DIC-
TATES PATHS ONE FOLLOWS.
(861)

NOTHING PERSONAL,
BUT, HAVE YOU REVIEWED YOUR HY-
GIENE OPTIONS LATELY?
(860)

NORMAL IS WHAT IT
IS, WHEN IT IS, WHERE IT IS.
AND THAT'S ALL IT IS.
(859)

TAKE A CHANCE, GO FOR
IT! IF YOU DON'T, YOU'LL HAVE NO-
THING TO SHOW FOR IT.
(858)

WHAT'S SADDER THAN LOS-
ING THE LOVE OF YOUR LIFE? NEV-
ER HAVING FOUND IT.
(854)

TRYING TO PLEASE ALL,
WHO GETS HURT THE MOST? YOU: THE
WOULD-BE PERFECT HOST.
(850)

BEST? GET IT DONE. DON'T
WAIT. THEM THAT WIN, JUMP IN. THEM
THAT DON'T HESITATE.
(847)

IT'S NOT THAT WE CAN'T
GET ALONG. JUST, FOR MOST, IF
ONE'S NOT STRONG, THEY'RE WRONG.
(846)

TRAIN YOUR BRAIN TO CON-
STRAIN THE BODY'S DESIRES TO
RE-KINDLE THOSE FIRES.
(844)

THIS HAS ALWAYS BEEN
CERTAIN: A FEW ARE WELL OFF,
THE REST ARE HURT'IN!
(838)

IF YOU FIND MOST TO
BE KIND IT'S BECAUSE, IN THEIR
MIND, YOU'RE NOT A THREAT.
(834)

AS A YOUTH, I FEARED
NOT GETTING. NOW, MUCH OLDER,
I FEAR FORGETTING.
(833)

MOST SEEK DIRECTION.
THEIR FEAR AND EMPTINESS MAKES
THEM NEED CONNECTION.
(831)

DON'T FALL FOR WOULD – COULD –
SHOULD. JUST GO WITH WHAT YOU SEE.
ALL ELSE IS MAYBE.
(820)

CHILDHOOD: WHEN WE'RE FREE.
ALL ELSE: PAYMENTS DUE AND RE-
SPONSIBILITY.
(811)

IF YOUR LIFE BECOMES
ROUTINE (MOST DO) KNOW THIS: YOU'RE
NO MACHINE … FIND YOU!
(805)

DROP THE PRETENSE. IN-
STEAD, FIND THE GOOD SENSE TO SAY
WHAT NEEDS TO BE SAID.
(803)

MEANING WELL WE RARELY
FOLLOW THROUGH – EVEN WHEN IT
BENEFITS US TOO.
(802)

SOME WANT TO CONFUSE,
SOME WANT TO USE, SOME TO ABUSE.
MOST WANT YOU TO LOSE.
(799)

KIDS PLAY ROUGH, BUT IT'S
NOT ADULT STUFF. LET ME KNOW
WHEN YOU'RE OLD ENOUGH.
(798)

WE'RE *"GOOD FRIENDS"* -- LONGTIME.
AS SUCH, IS IT ASKING TOO
MUCH TO KEEP IN TOUCH?
(797)

WE ALL HAVE UPS – DOWNS,
SMILES – FROWNS. FIND THE MEAN. STAY IN-
BETWEEN OUT OF BOUNDS.
(796)

PLAN A IS TO GET
ALONG. PLAN B'S TO SURVIVE
THOSE AGAINST PLAN A.
(795)

THE TWO BEST THINGS WE
CAN DO FOR ANYONE ARE
LISTEN AND ... LISTEN.
(791)

RARELY IS MONEY
NOT IN PLAY. IT PERMEATES
ALL WE DO EACH DAY.
(787)

NORMALCY IMPLIES
COMPLIANCE. ME? I WROTE THE
BOOK ON DEFIANCE.
(785)

DECEIT'S DOUBTS TAKE ROOT,
SPROUT, AS REASON'S CALM, OUT-SHOUTED,
RETREATS, IGNORED, ROUTED.
(784)

I'LL OBEY ANY
LAW – WHEN IT WORKS FOR ME. IF
NOT, WELL THEN – MAYBE.
(783)

ANDROGENOUS, ONES
NOT HOMOGENOUS, BUT
DOUBLY EROGENOUS.
(780)

MOST ARE MORE CONCERNED
ABOUT HOW THEY APPEAR, THAN
WHO THEY ARE. BIZARRE.
(766)

WHAT NONSENSE! SCREAMING
INNOCENCE, DAILY WE SELL
OUR INDEPENDENCE.
(754)

THOSE WHO CAN'T AGREE
TO DISAGREE WILL SURELY
SHARE IN TRAGEDY.
(753)

OUR TIME OF RECKON-
ING DOESN' COME AT OUR BECKON-
ING. WE'RE ALL ON CALL.
(749)

NOT CONTENT WITH LIFE'S
BUMPS AND DENTS MANY INVENT
MORE COMPLEX EVENTS.
(730)

AT SOME POINT WE HAVE
TO ASK OURSELVES, *"AM I IN
CHARGE OF ME – OR NOT?"*
(725)

FIND A WAY TO LIVE
WITH YOUR CHOICES THAT ALLOWS
YOU TO LEARN FROM THEM.
(723)

MOST TIMES WE IGNORE
RATIONAL AND POSSIBLE
FOR WANTING. MORE FUN.
(722)

OH! THE THINGS WE DO
TO GET OUT OF DOING THE
THINGS WE DON'T WANT TO.
(721)

WE PLAY GAMES IN OUR
MIND TO JUSTIFY OUR AC-
TIONS – OF ANY KIND.
(716)

RIGHT AND WRONG DEPEND
ON WHO YOU ARE, WHERE YOU ARE,
AND WHEN YOU ARE THERE.
(715)

KNOWING WHO WE ARE'S
ONE THING. THE BATTLE'S COMING
TO TERMS WITH THOSE THUTHS.
(714)

THERE'S NO RIGHT WAY OR
WRONG WAY. THERE'S YOUR WAY, MY WAY,
EACH WAY -- RIGHT OR WRONG.
(712)

HOW MUCH YOU KNOW IS
PROPORTIONAL TO HOW MUCH
YOU KNOW YOU DON'T KNOW.
(711)

MY LIFE'S TOO GOOD. WHAT'S
THE CATCH? AIN'T NOTHING FREE. HOW
MUCH WILL IT COST ME?
(709)

SEEKING MEANING AND
PURPOSE IN LIFE IS BEST SERVED
SEARCHING WITHIN YOU.
(708)

YES, YOU'RE QUITE RIGHT TO
BE WARY. LIFE'S ROUGH, SCARY,
SO ARBITRARY.
(707)

IF YOU CAN'T KEEP THE
PROMISES YOU MAKE TO YOUR-
SELF, THINK YOU'LL HAVE FRIENDS?
(705)

TELL US BOTH SIDES – ALL
YOU CAN FIND. HIDE NOTHING. WE'LL
MAKE UP OUR OWN MINDS.
(704)

THERE'S NO *"I CAN'T DO
THIS IN YOU."* THAT'S YOUR GREATEST
STRENGTH AND CERTAIN DOOM.
(701)

THE TRICK IS TO GET
WHAT YOU WANT WITHOUT SEEMING
TO KNOW YOU'RE TRYING.
(700)

JUST WHEN WE THINK *"I'VE
ARRIVED!"*, WE SCREW UP. LIFE. TWO
STEPS FORWARD; ONE BACK.
(698)

VERY FEW THINGS ARE AS
EASY AS IT SEEMS. SORRY:
ONLY IN YOUR DREAMS.
(689)

HEED THIS TALE OF WOE:
SOON, THE MANY 'WITHOUT' WILL
BRING THOSE 'WITH' DOWN LOW.
(688)

LIFE'S PASSAGE TAKES MOST
BY SURPRISE, ILL-PREPARED FOR
SO MUCH COMPROMISE.
(685)

GIFTED, BOOKSMART, THESE DON'T
COMPENSATE FOR YOUR LACK OF
IMMAGINATION.
(683)

OH, YE TIMID SOULS!
KNOW YE NOT 'TIS THE BOLD WHO
ATTAIN LIFE'S TREASURES?
(675)

THE ANSWERS YOU'RE SEEK-
ING ARE ONLY AS GOOD AS
THE QUESTIONS YOU ASK
(672)

THERE'S NO DESIGNER
MORALITY – THIS FITS, THAT
DOESN'T. ONE SIZE FITS ALL.
(671)

WITH AGE, LIFE'S MYSTER-
IES FADE. BY THEN WE'RE IN THRALL
TO LIFE CHOICES MADE.
(668)

WHAT WE EXPECT FROM
OTHERS IS OFTEN MORE THAN
WE'D EXPECT OF US.
(667)

WHEN WINNING'S YOUR AIM
ALL'S FAIR. THERE'S NOTHING TO BLAME
FOR HOW YOU GOT THERE.
(665)

PLAYING BY THE RULES
WILL GET YOU A GOLD WATCH, IF
YOU'RE LUCKY. MINE RUSTED.
(663)

EMPATHY EXACTS
PAYMENT, BUT ITS ABSENCE IS
WHAT'S WRONG WITH THIS WORLD.
(662)

CONFIDENCE COMES WITH
EXPERIENCE, WHICH COMES FROM
FAILURE. YOU LEARN QUICK.
(661)

MOST CHOOSE TO BE NOT
WRONG, RATHER THAN 'RIGHT', SO
THEY DON'T SAY ANYTHING.
(660)

LIFE'S A TUG-OF-WAR:
HELP OTHERS? YOURSELF? WHO? WHEN?
HOW? CONSTANT STRUGGLE.
(650)

WHEN TALKING TO SOME-
ONE WHO WON'T LOOK YOU IN THE
EYE, STOP, SAY *"GOOD-BYE."*
(648)

IN ONE EAR, OUT THE
OTHER; THAT'S HOW WE LISTEN
TO ONE ANOTHER.
(641)

THE WORST SINS ARE OF
OMMISSION; KNOWING, BUT NOT
ACTING; APATHY.
(637)

SO, YOU'RE SURE LIFE HAS
PURPOSE? WHO AM I TO SHAT-
TER YOUR DELUSIONS?
(632)

TAKING OTHERS AND
THINGS FOR GRANTED WILL COME BACK TO
HAUNT AND CONFOUND YOU.
(631)

WHY CAN'T PEOPLE GET
ALONG? SIMPLE: SOME OF US
GROW UP, MOST GROW OLD.
(630)

THE HEART DIES SLOWLY,
ONE HOPE AT A TIME; TOO LATE
WE LEARN HOPE'S A DREAM.
(629)

EXPECT THE UNEX-
PECTED. LIFE'S LIKE THAT. DON'T GET RILED.
JUST EASE INTO IT.
(627)

EVEN WITH HARD WORK
THERE'S LITTLE CHANCE THAT HONEST
PEOPLE WILL GET RICH.
(625)

LEFT-HANDED, RIGHT BRAINED, THE
DIVERGENCE BEGINS EARLY,
INCREASES YEARLY.
(624)

YOU'RE TOUGHER THAN YOU
THINK. TOO BAD IT TAKES HARD TIMES
TO REALIZE IT.
(622)

RESPONSIBLE? MA-
TURE? OF COURSE -- JUST DON'T LET GO
OF YOUR INNER CHILD.
(621)

ALL YOU GOTTA DO
TO GET IN TROUBLE THESE DAYS
IS OPEN YOUR MOUTH.
(619)

WORRYING ABOUT
WHAT PEOPLE THINK ASSURES THAT
YOU'LL NEVER BE YOU.
(617)

IF THINGS FALL APART
ASK YOURSELF *"WHAT HURTS WORSE,
MY EGO OR MY HEART?"*
(616)

"IT'S COMPLICATED", MEANS
EITHER *"I DON'T KNOW"* OR *"I'M
NOT GONNA TELL YOU."*
(615)

TOO MUCH FREEDOM'S SELF-
ISH; NOT ENOUGH DEADENS ONE'S
SOUL. TREAD THAT FINE LINE.
(614)

THAT DREAM OF SHARING
THE WEALTH WILL NEVER BE. THE
HAVES WON'T ALLOW IT.
(610)

SO, YOU'RE WAITING FOR
LOVE, TRUE AND PERFECT. WASTE
OF TIME. SETTLE FOR TRUE.
(607)

GIVING UP – EASY.
LIVING, FINDING FULFILLMENT,
HAPPINESS – TOUGH STUFF.
(604)

SOME WATCH FROM THE FRINGE,
SEEING AND HEARING MUCH THAT
GAMERS OVERLOOK.
(595)

BEING AFRAID TO
FAIL KEEPS YOU FROM TRYING – WHICH
IS WORSE THAN FAILING.
(587)

NOTHING IN LIFE'S FREE.
ONE DAY YOUR BILL WILL COME DUE.
HOW MUCH DO YOU OWE?
(584)

HERE'S THE TRUTH, THE WHOLE
TRUTH, AND NOTHING BUT THE TRUTH:
EVERYONE LIES.
(583)

IN THE BASE OF YOUR
BRAIN, PRIMITIVE, SUBCONSCIOUS
INSTINCTS HAVE FREE REIGN.
(581)

WE DON'T SEE OR HEAR
THE SAME THINGS OTHERS DO, EX-
CEPT WHEN WE WANT TO.
(580)

WAITING FOR SOMETHING
TO HAPPEN IN YOUR LIFE? ALL
THAT GETS YOU IS OLD.
(578)

IF THERE'S NO CONSCIENCE
OR COMPASSION, ALL THAT'S LEFT
IS SORROW AND LOSS.
(577)

BEING FRIENDLY YET
ENIGMATIC KEEPS THEM GUESS-
ING – AND OFF YOUR BACK.
(574)

PLOTTERS PLOT. SCHEMERS
SCHEME. LIARS LIE. HONESTY
REQUIRES GREAT COURAGE.
(572)

THE RIGHT WAY IS THE
WINNER'S WAY. THE WRONG WAY WAS
THE ONE THAT DIDN'T WIN.
(571)

AS FOR THE COUNT OF
MAN'S INHUMANITY TO
MAN, GUILTY AS CHARGED.
(570)

FORGIVING'S ONE THING.
FORGETTING'S QUITE DIFFERENT.
IT'S IMPOSSIBLE.
(569)

WE CAN NEVER TRU-
LY KNOW ANOTHER PERSON --
THOUGH WE BELIEVE SO.
(567)

ASYMETRICAL,
LIFE'S NOT CENTERED, BALANCED OR
EVEN. THAT'S WHAT'S FUN!
(564)

THE CONSEQUENCE OF
HAVING NO CONSCIOUS IS NOT
TRUSTING ANYONE.
(563)

INCOMPREHENSI-
BLY, MOST ACCEPT MEDIOC-
RITY AS THEIR DUE.
(562)

IN TODAY'S LEXI-
CON *"FOREVER"* MEANS HOW LONG
WHO SAID IT, SAYS SO.
(560)

ALL DEALS HAVE ONE SA-
CROSANCT ELEMENT: *"WHAT DO
I GET OUT OF IT?"*
(559)

MOST OF US GO WITH
FIRST IMPRESSIONS. THAT'S WHY WE
OFTEN GET IT WRONG.
(558)

ART STIMULATES, MAKES
US THINK, CAUSES US TO RE-
ACT, TO GET INVOLVED.
(554)

YOU CAN CRY, DEAR CHILD.
EVEN WHEN YOU'RE OLD IT HURTS
TO BE MADE FUN OF.
(545)

BEING BLATANTLY
BLASPHEMOUS BENEFITS BOLD,
BLARNEY BLESSED BEINGS.
(544)

TOO MUCH OF A GOOD
THING SPOILS US. WE FORGET WHAT
THOSE HARD TIMES WERE LIKE.
(543)

ELEVATED EGOS
EXHIBIT EGREGEOUS ETH-
ICAL EVASIONS.
(540)

THERE'S A LOT TO BE
SAID FOR AVOIDING CONFLICT.
NO ONE'S LISTENING.
(536)

CHILDREN KNOW RIGHT FROM
WRONG. ADULTS KNOW WHAT'S RIGHT FOR
THEM IS NEVER WRONG.
(534)

WE GET DESPERATE.
FEAR TAKES OVER. USE IT TO
BREAK OUT, NOT WITHDRAW.
(533)

WHEN YOU'RE ON A HOT
DOG BUDGET WITH LOBSTER DREAMS,
SLEEP LESS, WORK HARDER.
(530)

MIND OVER MATTER?
NEVER MIND. DOESN'T MATTER.
WHAT COUNTS IS WHAT'S RIGHT.
(529)

HARD TO KNOW WHAT MOST
PEOPLE WANT THESE DAYS. FEW SAY.
BE SURE OF YOURSELF.
(528)

WANT AN EASY LIFE?
LISTEN. SAY WHAT YOU MEAN. MEAN
WHAT YOU SAY. LISTEN.
(526)

WITH TOO MUCH, MOST GET
GREEDY. WITH TOO LITTLE, MOST
ARE NEEDY. LOSE – LOSE.
(520)

"SOPHISTICATES" SAY,
AND DO, WHAT IT TAKES. WE CRUDE
ONE'S DO WHAT WE SAY.
(518)

MAN'S NATURE IS TO
WANT, GET MORE – HAVE IT ALL. HOW?
PRIMARILY WAR.
(517)

SOME WILL TAKE YOU DOWN
'CAUSE THEY CAN. MOST DO IT TO
BOOST THEIR SELF-ESTEEM.
(516)

WHAT TO DO? FAITH'S LOVE
AND COMPASSION ARE OFTEN
AT REASON'S EXPENSE.
(515)

THERE'S THINGS THAT MUST BE
DONE YOU JUST DON'T WANT TO DO.
LET WISDOM PREVAIL.
(513)

IT'S O.K. TO SHARE
YOUR OPINIONS – WHEN REQUESTED.
OTHERWISE, BEST NOT.
(512)

WHAT'S OBVIOUS TO
YOU ISN'T TO OTHERS, AND VICE-
VERSA. WE CAN LEARN.
(511)

BEING HIGH BORN OR
LUCKY DOESN'T MAKE YOU SPECIAL.
THAT YOU HAVE TO EARN.
(510)

NEVER BE SO SURE
OF YOURSELF THAT YOU FORGET
TO COVER YOUR SIX.
(509)

PIED PIPER TOOT YOUR
FLUTE. NOT HARD TO FIND LOTS OF
LEMMINGS ANYWHERE.
(508)

IN A BETTER WORLD,
WE'D GET ALONG, LIVE IN PEACE.
NO CHANCE THAT'LL HAPPEN.
(506)

WANT TO WIN? DON'T LET
YOUR FOE(S) KNOW WHO YOU ARE. THEY
WON'T SEE YOU COMING.
(505)

LIVING LARGE: WHAT'S RIGHT
GETS BLURRED. SCRAPING BY: SPIRIT'S
CRUSHED. FIND A BETWEEN.
(504)

WHEN YOU MAKE A MESS
OUT OF LIFE, *"FESS UP"*, THEN
GET GOING – CLEAN IT UP.
(499)

LIFE'S ANCIENT RHYTHMS
HAVE BEEN ABANDONED BY US
IN OUR LUST FOR *"NOW"!*
(498)

WHEN YOU'RE WITH SOMEONE –
REALLY WITH SOMEONE – YOU STEP
BACK AND LET THEM SHINE.
(497)

DON'T TRY TO JUSTI-
FY YOUR BELIEFS TO OTHERS.
HAVE FAITH IN YOURSELF!
(494)

SOME PEOPLE SAY AND
DO OFF THE WALL THINGS, JUST TO
SEE WHAT MIGHT HAPPEN.
(492)

STOP FRETTING OVER
WHAT MIGHT BE. GET OUT THERE AND
DISCOVER WHAT IS!
(491)

THINK YOU'RE PRETTIER,
SMARTER, BETTER? VAIN FOOL. WE'RE
ALL TEMPORARY.
(490)

SPORATIC INTER-
VALS OF DOWNTIME DO WONDERS
FOR ONE'S ATTITUDE.
(489)

ONLY ONE THING'S CERTAIN:
WE'RE NOT GETTING OUT ALIVE.
GO FOR IT. HANG TEN.
(488)

IT'S A FINE PRINT, HACKED,
BOTTOM LINE WORLD. BE CAUTIOUS,
WARY, PREEMPTIVE.
(487)

THE ONE WE THINK'S *"THE
ONE"* MIGHT BE – TODAY. BEYOND
THAT NO GUARANTEE.
(485)

ALWAYS DOING THE
RIGHT THING REMINDS OTHERS THEY
DON'T. GUESS WHO THEY BLAME?
(484)

NEVER BEING SAT-
ISFIED LEADS TO ONE CONCLU-
SION: YOU'VE GOT PROBLEMS.
(480)

IF WE ALLOW OUR-
SELVES TO BE VULNERABLE,
GOOD THINGS WILL HAPPEN.
(479)

THE CALM OF CHAOS
IS OFTEN EASIER THAN
FACING OUR DEMONS.
(476)

LOVE'S THE EASY PART.
GETTING ALONG, STAYING TO-
GETHER, THAT'S HARD WORK.
(475)

GOOD INTENTIONS NOT
ACTED ON ARE LIKE AN OLD JUNK
DRAWER FULL OF DREAMS.
(473)

STUPIDITY'S WORSE
THAN IGNORANCE: YOU KNOW IT'S
WRONG, BUT KEEP GOING.
(472)

FEELING DOWN, CONFUSED,
UNCERTAIN? TAKE A HARD LOOK
AT THE REST OF US.
(471)

THERE ARE TIMES WHEN YOU
HAVE TO SAY *"IT'S NOT RIGHT, IT'S
NOT WRONG. IT JUST IS."*
(470)

FOR PEACE OF MIND TRY
NOT TO BELIEVE EVERY-
THING THAT YOU'RE THINKING.
(469)

HEY! YOU ALWAYS KNOW
WHAT YOU'RE DOING: WHATEVER
IS REQUIRED TO WIN.
(468)

WE CAN'T HELP WHO WE
LOVE. BUT WE CAN HELP KNOWING
IF THEY'RE RIGHT FOR US.
(467)

BELIEVE IN YOURSELF.
PUT YOURSELF OUT THERE. DON'T BACK
DOWN. BE PROACTIVE.
(459)

CONSIDER THIS OF
THOSE LESS FORTUNATE: ABSENT
GOOD LUCK, THAT IS ME.
(455)

LIFE HAS ITS RHYTHMS –
EBBS AND FLOWS. RECOGNIZE THEM,
DANCE WITH EACH IN TUNE.
(454)

HAPPINESS IS IN-
TERNAL: YOU ACCEPTING, AND
TRUSTING, WHO YOU ARE.
(453)

SHUNNING THE PAST RISKS
REPEATING, AND ENLARGING,
ALL IT'S EXCESSES.
(452)

LOTS OF US DON'T HES-
ITATE, TO EXAGERATE OUR LIVES,
EASE THE NUMBNESS.
(449)

KNOWING SOMETHINGS WRONG,
NOT TRYING TO CHANGE IT, IS
WORSE THAN NOT KNOWING.
(448)

OUR DIFFERENCES
MAKE US STRONGER. LET'S SHARE THEM
TO BETTER US ALL.
(446)

MOST OF US DON'T ASK
FOR HELP. PRIDE, MAINLY, AND IT'S
TWIN, EMBARRASSMENT.
(444)

WOMEN REFLECT, THEN
ACT. MEN ACT, THEN MAYBE RE-
FLECT, MOSTLY REGRET.
(443)

LIARS FIGURE, BUT
FIGURES DON'T LIE. WHAT'S TO
BELIEVE? GO FIGURE!
(442)

DON'T LOSE WHO YOU ARE
TRYING TO FIT INTO A
LIFE YOU KNOW'S NOT RIGHT.
(440)

KINDNESS OF SPIRIT,
GENEROSITY OF HEART:
THESE SHOULD GUIDE OUR LIVES.
(439)

MOST WON'T ASK THEMSELVES
THE HARD QUESTIONS 'CAUSE THEY'RE A-
FRAID OF THE ANSWERS.
(436)

IF YOU LET OTHERS
TAKE ADVANTAGE OF YOU THEY
WILL, EVERY TIME.
(430)

NO ONE, NOTHING, CAN
MAKE YOU HAPPY BUT YOU. GIVE
YOURSELF PERMISSION.
(428)

TWO THINGS I LEARNED IN
GRADE SCHOOL: MIGHT IS RIGHT; IF YOU
DON'T PAY, YOU CAN'T PLAY.
(427)

WOMEN INTERNAL-
IZE. MEN EXTERNALIZE: WITH
FEW, RARE, EXCEPTIONS.
(426)

YOU CAN'T TRUST PEOPLE
WHO GO AROUND TELLING YOU
NOT TO TRUST PEOPLE.
(422)

WE CAN'T CONTROL WHAT
OTHERS SAY OR DO – JUST HOW
WE REACT TO THEM.
(416)

SWEET CHILD! THINK YOU'VE GOT
PROBLEMS? WAIT 'TIL YOU GROW UP
AND YOU ARE ON YOUR OWN.
(415)

IF THE FUTURE'S US,
AS WE ARE NOW, THEN GOD HELP
OUR INHERITORS.
(407)

YOU CHOOSE WHO YOU ARE.
WHAT YOU DO AND WHO YOU'RE WITH
FOLLOW SUIT. THINK HARD.
(405)

UPS – DOWNS; WINS – LOSSES;
A FEW LARGE EVENTS – DAILY
GRIND. LIFE. EMBRACE IT!
(402)

NO ONE'S COMPLETELY
HONEST OR OBJECTIVE. BUT,
MOST CAN'T ADMIT IT.
(400)

WHEN YOU'RE YOUNG, TIME CREEPS
LIKE GLACIERS. PASSING MIDDLE
AGE, IT'S AT LIGHT SPEED.
(398)

GOT TO GET OVER
YOURSELF BEFORE ANYONE
CAN GET THROUGH TO YOU.
(391)

IF ALL GOES WELL, WE'LL
HAVE MORE GOOD TIMES THAN BAD ONES,
MORE GLAD THAN SAD DAYS.
(390)

TEMPT ME NOT WITH LUST
OR LUCRE. PERSUADE ME WITH
REASON AND PASSION.
(389)

MY CONDOLENCES
TO ALL WHO BELIEVE GOOD WILL
MATTERS. IF ONLY ...
(383)

SOMETIMES IT'S BEST TO
SAY NOTHING AT ALL. SILENCE
SPEAKS LOUDLY, CLEARLY.
(382)

MOM AND DAD, LOVE YOUR
CHILDREN, BUT HAVE ENOUGH LEFT
OVER FOR YOURSELVES.
(381)

AT TIMES, WE GET HUNG
UP ON A WORD, INSTEAD OF
GRASPING ITS INTENT.
(376)

AT THE END, LET'S HOPE
IT'S SAID THEY DID THEIR BEST AND
NEVER, EVER QUIT.
(374)

MOST OF US ARE SLAVES
TO CONVENIENCE, RATHER
THAN MAKE THE HARD CHOICE.
(371)

SEEING THE GRAYS IN
THIS BLACK/WHITE TECH WORLD BACKLIGHTS
AND ISOLATES US.
(365)

PLANNING'S NEEDED. RE-
FLECTION BIRTHS WISDOM. LIVING'S
PRESENT TENSE ONLY!
(355)

EARTH TO DREAMERS: THE
GRASS IS THE SAME COLOR ON
BOTH SIDES OF THAT FENCE.
(354)

SAD FACT OF LIFE: TRUTH
TAKES BOTTOM RUNG TO RUMOR,
HEARSAY AND GOSSIP.
(353)

EXPAND YOUR COMFORT
ZONE REGULARLY. DON'T BE
CONTENT WITH THE KNOWN.
(352)

FEELING SORRY FOR
YOURSELF WASTES TIME: IT IMPEDES
YOUR FORWARD PROGRESS.
(351)

MOST OF US WOULD DO
BETTER IF WE COULD JUST GET
OUT OF OUR OWN WAY.
(350)

BY WHATEVER MEANS,
THERE'S NOT MUCH SADDER THAN A
CHILD'S LOST INNOCENCE.
(347)

IT IS VITAL TO
MATTER TO SOMEONE. IF NOT
YOUR LIFE'S MEANINGLESS.
(345)

NOTHING WILL HAPPEN
FOR YOU UNTIL YOU'RE PREPARED
FOR IT. GET READY!
(343)

FAMILY, OFTEN
TAKEN FOR GRANTED, SHOULD BE
CHERISHED – REGARDLESS.
(341)

OTHERS WON'T FEEL GOOD
ABOUT YOU UNTIL YOU FEEL
GOOD ABOUT YOURSELF.
(340)

THERE'LL COME A TIME WHEN
YOU ACCEPT YOU KNOW A LOT
LESS THAN YOU THOUGHT. WOE!
(338)

SET ME FREE. LET ME
CHOOSE WHO I WANT TO BE. RE-
LEASE. HAVE FAITH IN ME.
(336)

SHARING OUR FAILURES
WITH A FRIEND MIGHT PREVENT THEM
FROM TAKING THAT FALL.
(335)

WE KNOW WHAT WE SHOULD
DO. NOT DOING IT KEEPS US
AT EACH OTHER'S THROATS.
(334)

CAN'T FIX EVERY-
THING. GOT TO ACCEPT DEFEAT
AT TIMES. THAT'S JUST LIFE.
(333)

EVIL'S INTENDED. IT'S
MEANS DESIGNED TO ACHIEVE ONE
END: TOTAL CONTROL.
(331)

SCHEDULE VIRUS CHECKS
OF YOU: SCAN; DELETE; UPGRADE;
REPROGRAM; REBOOT.
(330)

IS THIS TOO MUCH TO
ASK? PUT YOURSELF IN MY PLACE
FIRST, THEN PASS SENTENCE.
(329)

RAISED TO FOLLOW THE
RULES, FEW DO. THESE ARE HELD IN
CONTEMPT BY THE *"DON'TS"*.
(327)

BEST ADVICE I'VE HEARD
IN YEARS: *"NEVER MISS A CHANCE TO
SHUT UP"* – LISTEN!
(325)

TRUST YOUR INSTINCTS. THEY
KNOW YOU BETTER THAN YOU KNOW
YOURSELF. KEEP THEM CLOSE.
(323)

POLITICS PERVADES
ALL THING'S HUMAN. OUR LIVES ARE
AGENDA SUBTEXTS.
(322)

GETTING WHAT WE WANT'S
NOT NEAR AS EXCITING AS
WANTING TO GET IT.
(321)

LIKE GAMES? KNOW THE RULES,
PLAYERS, YOUR LIMITS. TIMING'S
THE KEY. PLAN, WAIT, POUNCE!
(320)

MOST PEOPLE DON'T
HEAR WHAT YOU SAY, ONLY WHAT THEY
THINK YOU SAID ... BIG DIFF!
(319)

LIKE TO TALK A LOT?
MAKE SURE YOUR MEMORY'S SHARP.
WORDS SOMETIMES BITE BACK.
(318)

KEEP THINGS SIMPLE. NO
LIES, NO SCHEMES – GOOD OLE' STRAIGHT AND
NARROW. HARD TO DO.
(316)

SO, GETTING WHAT YOU
WANT WILL MAKE YOU CONTENT? *R-I-G-H-T!*
THERE'S NEVER *"ENOUGH"*.
(314)

TO BE SAFE WE HIDE
BEHIND PERSONAS THAT BLIND
US TO OTHER'S TRUTHS.
(313)

FINDING A REASON
TO SMILE AND LAUGH EACH DAY HELPS
CHASE SELF-DOUBT AWAY.
(307)

LIFE'S NUMBER ONE RULE?
<u>NEVER</u> <u>QUIT</u>! ALWAYS FINISH
WHAT YOU START, OR LOSE!
(303)

ANATOMY'S NOT
DESTINY, JUST WHAT YOU ARE.
YOU CHOOSE WHO YOU ARE.
(302)

"A LITTLE BIT OF
SOMETHING IS BETTER THAN A
WHOLE LOT OF NOTHING."
(298)

BEING SMART AND GOOD
ISN'T ALWAYS ENOUGH. YOU'VE GOT
TO BE LUCKY, TOO.
(297)

MOST FUN THINGS IN LIFE
AREN'T PLANNED. KEEP AN OPEN MIND.
MAKE ROOM FOR SURPRISE.
(296)

MOST OF US WILL RE-
ARRANGE FACTS TO SUIT OUR ENDS –
NEVERMIND THEIR TRUTH(S).
(292)

EVERY EFFORT
SHOULDN'T BE *"DO OR DIE"*, JUST
YOUR BEST AT THAT TIME.
(288)

WHAT'S YOUR 'WHY' -- MAKES YOU
LAUGH, CRY, SOAR, SIGH? IT'S UNIQUE,
YOUR'S ALONE. FIND IT.
(284)

HIGHEST HIGH? POWER.
MONEY, SEX? – NOT EVEN CLOSE.
ONE TASTE, HOOKED FOR LIFE.
(282)

TO ENJOY LIFE MORE --
HIDE PHONES; SCREENS OFF; GO OUTSIDE;
MEET PEOPLE; TALK! HUG!
(280)

LIFE'S DICHOTOMY:
LOVE, KIDS, FAMILY AND/OR
MONEY, LUST, POWER.
(276)

GAME PLAN: SAY WHAT I
HAVE TO SAY; GET IT OUT THERE;
SHUT UP. FADE AWAY.
(275)

WHEN YOU SELL OTHERS
SHORT, OFTEN THEY'LL SURPRISE YOU.
SO, -- GIVE 'EM SOME SLACK!
(274)

LIFE AIN'T FAIR. NEVER
WILL BE. GOT TO MAKE IT UN-
FAIR IN YOUR FAVOR.
(273)

GIVE ME EMOTIONS
OVER LOGIC ANYTIME.
FEELINGS ROUSE ACTIONS.
(269)

DO YOU WANT A LOT
OF *"FRIENDS"*, OR ONE OR TWO, WHO
LOVE AND RESPECT YOU?
(268)

IS MY BAD YOUR BAD,
YOUR GOOD MY GOOD? PLEASE! SAY NO!
VIVE LA DIFFERENCE!!
(267)

EGO'S OUR DOWNFALL.
TOO LITTLE CAUSES DISPAIR;
TOO MUCH ISOLATES.
(265)

LIFE. THE GREATEST GIFT.
THE ONE WE TAKE FOR GRANTED –
UNTIL IT'S TOO LATE.
(263)

CROSS YOUR T'S; DOT YOUR
I'S. FOLLOW THE RULES. WHAT FOR?
WISE UP! NO ON CARES.
(260)

PUTTING IT MILDLY:
IT'S MOSTLY "ME", NOT MUCH "WE"
THESE DAYS GLOBALLY.
(257)

YEAH! NICE TO GET WHAT
YOU WANT. JUST BE SURE YOU WANT
WHAT YOU'RE GONNA GET.
(252)

FEELING SORRY FOR
YOURSELF ONLY DELAYS THE
PROBLEM'S SOLUTION.
(251)

IT'S ESSENTIAL TO
EMBRACE YOUR UNIQUENESS IF
YOU HOPE TO FIND PEACE.
(250)

IN A CRUNCH, TOO MUCH
THINKING DELAYS RESPONSE TIME.
BE READY. FOCUS.
(249)

SELF-ADVERTISING
REIGNS; HUMILITY, GRACE ARE
GHOSTS TO TODAY'S YOUTH.
(248)

THINGS DON'T JUST HAPPEN.
WE'RE RESPONSIBLE FOR OUR
ACTIONS. IT'S ON YOU.
(246)

THE BEST WAY TO WIN:
DECEIVE, CASTING SEEDS OF DOUBT,
DIVIDE AND CONQUER.
(245)

BELIEVING SOMETHING'S
TRUE DOESN'T MAKE IT SO. BUT, ...
WHO'S DEFINING TRUTH?
(244)

HOW TO SUCCEED? DON'T
DWELL ON THE PROBABLE. DEAL
WITH WHAT'S POSSIBLE.
(243)

GOING, GOING, GONE!
TOO SOON WE'RE OLD. TOO LATE SMART.
DON'T DAWDLE. PLAN. ACT.
(242)

WE CAN BE MENDED:
WISDOM, ACCEPTANCE STICHED TIGHT
WITH COMPASSION'S THREADS.
(241)

WHY WORK TO SOLVE YOUR
TROUBLES? THERE'S A BETTER WAY.
IT'S CALLED: DRUG OF CHOICE.
(240)

IT'S NOT WHAT WE SAY
OR WHO WE THINK WE ARE. WHAT
WE DO DEFINES US.
(239)

"LIFE IS BUT A DREAM"
IN NO TIME WE WAKE UP
TO FIND ITS PAST US BY.
(238)

LIFE ISN'T LINEAR.
IT'S CURVED AND WARPED. LOGIC'S A
MAN-MADE CRUTCH FOR HOPE.
(237)

MY FERVENT HOPE IS
THAT MY CHILDREN HAVE HEALTHY,
HAPPY, LOVE FILLED LIVES.
(232)

I MAY NOT BE THE
SMARTEST, BUT, IF I WORK HARD,
I CAN BE THE BEST.
(231)

WE HAVE SOLUTIONS.
WE NEED PEOPLE TO AGREE,
THEN WORK TOGETHER.
(230)

FAILURE TO LISTEN
CLOSELY AND HASTY JUDGMENT
MAKE CONFLICT CERTAIN.
(226)

TRUST BETRAYED RARELY
REGAINS ITS TREASURED STATUS.
KEEP YOUR PROMISES.
(225)

WE FIGHT PITCHED BATTLES
FOR OUR SELF-GAIN. WISH WE'D FIGHT
AS HARD FOR US ALL.
(221)

LONELINESS OPENS
US TO PARANOID SELF-DOUBT
WHICH CRUSHES THE HEART.
(220)

ENVY; JEALOUSY –
VILE TWINS CONCEIVED IN THE MIND,
ROTTING ONE'S SOUL.
(218)

DON'T *"VISIT"* IN AISLES,
EXITS OR ENTRIES. BE KIND,
BE CONSIDERATE.
(215)

IF YOUR HAPPINESS
STEMS FROM OTHERS YOU'LL HAVE A
ROLLER-COASTER LIFE.
(214)

LAWYERS DO THIS: CHOOSE
EACH WORD FOR ITS MEANING. READ
THE FINE PRINT. GOOD LUCK!
(209)

MY KIDS MEAN THE WORLD
TO ME. ALAS, MY MONEY
MEANS THE WORLD TO THEM.
(208)

ASSUMING, PRIOR
TO CORROBORATION, EARNS
YOU THE DONKEY'S TAIL!
(205)

PERFECTIONS PURSUIT
BRINGS ONE SORROWS, FRUSTRATION
AND LIFETIME MALAISE.
(203)

DENIAL EASES
PAIN, BUT PREVENTS WHAT'S NEEDED:
FACING THE PROBLEM.
(200)

WORK ALL DAY, BY NIGHT
PLAY? LIV'N LARGE? ... TIME LURKS, GRINNING.
SOON PIPER SCREAMS "PAY!"
(193)

AT TIMES, A LITTLE'S
JUST RIGHT – SATISFYING, BUT
NOT OVERWHELMING.
(190)

THE DELUSION WE'RE
FREE, IN CONTROL, BRINGS HOPE THAT
CANNOT BE FULFILLED.
(189)

SPIRIT STRONG? FLESH WEAK?
ONE OF LIFE'S TRIBULATIONS.
HOLD BACK? GIVE IN? CHOICE.
(188)

MOST DRIVERS IGNORE
SPEED LAWS AND COMMON SENSE YET
ARE SHOCKED WHEN THEY CRASH.
(184)

WHAT'S YOUR HEART QUOTIENT?
HOW WILL YOU BE REMEMBERED?
LOVED? OR NOT AT ALL?
(181)

BEING NICE IS HARD.
THERE ARE TOO FEW EXAMPLES
OF CONSCIOUS KINDNESS.
(180)

DOES LIFE HAVE PURPOSE?
IF YES, WE SHOULD *ALL* SHARE IT.
IF NO, WHAT THE F--K?
(178)

FOR SOME, ODD IS ODD.
FOR OTHERS, ODD SEEMS NORMAL.
HOW ODD ALL THIS IS.
(172)

MOSTLY, WE ONLY
SEE WHAT WE WANT TO SEE ... THE
HUMAN CONDITION.
(170)

WINNING REQUIRES THE
WISDOM GAINED BY FAILING. WE
LEARN HOW NOT TO LOSE.
(169)

THINGS GOING BADLY?
IT'S WORSE THAN YOU THINK! GUESS WHY.
YOU'VE GOT NO CONTROL.
(167)

KEY TO SUCCEEDING?
IT'S NOT HARD – SIMPLE IN FACT:
PLAN; SHOW UP; WORK! WORK!
(166)

AFRAID TO REACH OUT,
ADMIT YOU NEED HELP? GUESS WHAT?
YOU'RE NOT ALONE FRIEND.
(164)

WANT TO BE HAPPY?
LOSE THE DELUSION OF LIFE
BEING SERIOUS.
(163)

WE EACH HAVE TO FIND
OUR OWN HARMONY WITH LIFE
THAT'S UNIQUE TO US.
(162)

WHEN OUR BACK'S TO THE
WALL, WE'LL DO ALMOST ANYTHING:
SURVIVAL INSTINCT.
(159)

NOTHING'S NEW. WE ALL
BORROW, COPY, IMITATE.
MAKE IT WORK FOR YOU.
(158)

COINCIDENTAL
MEANS: I HAVEN'T HAD TIME
TO THINK OF AN EXCUSE.
(157)

CHANGE IS A GIVEN.
ADAPT OR GET LEFT BEHIND.
NO OTHER OPTIONS.
(153)

DON'T BE THINKIN' YOU
GOT PLENTY OF TIME. NOT SO –
TIME *ALWAYS* RUNS OUT.
(151)

MURPHY'S LAW: IF IT
CAN GO WRONG, IT WILL. MY TAKE?
MURPH'S AN OPTIMIST!
(148)

FATE IMPLIES PLANNING,
ORDER; ALL IS FORETOLD, HELP!
GOOD LUCK! WE NEED IT!
(147)

CHAOS ATTRIBUTES
ALL TO RANDOM ACTS. IF SO,
CHILL! ENJOY THE RIDE.
(146)

WHEN REASON CONFRONTS
FAITH, THE MOST LIKELY OUTCOME?
FAITH TRUMPS REASON'S DOUBTS.
(145)

HOW TO KNOW SOMEONE:
THUMBS DOWN; TURN HEAD; LOOK AT THEM;
NOW, BEGIN SPEAKING.
(144)

"ALL ENDS WELL." HOW? I
CAN'T SAY. *"IT'S A MYSTERY."*
HAVE FAITH. PERSEVERE.
(143)

MALE/FEMALE. WHAT'S THE
DIFF? A FEW HORMONES. THE REST'S
LEARNED SOCIAL BIAS.
(142)

WE COME IN ALONE.
TRYING TO FIT, WE PASS THROUGH.
WE GO OUT ALONE.
(141)

EVERY DAY IS A
WINDING ROAD: CURVES, STOPS, TRAFFIC.
EYES SHARP! STAY ALERT.
(140)

DO YOU TRUST YOUR FRIENDS?
CAN YOU COUNT ON THEM? WHICH ONES?
JUST THINK ABOUT IT.
(139)

YOU CAN BELIEVE THIS:
"NO GOOD DEED GOES UNPUNISHED"
IT'S SO TRUE, SAD TOO.
(138)

FEELING ENTITLED?
THINK THIS WORLD OWES YOU SOMETHING?
WE GET WHAT WE EARN.
(137)

CAN'T QUITE COMPREHEND
WHY PEOPLE DO WHAT THEY DO?
FOLLOW THE MONEY!
(136)

WHERE IS IT WRITTEN
THAT SKIN COLOR DETERMINES
A PERSON'S STATUS?
(135)

HOPE MEANS YOU'RE ALIVE,
YOU HAVEN'T GIVEN UP – YET.
WITHOUT IT LIFE'S DONE.
(134)

IT TAKES MORE COURAGE
TO WALK AWAY FROM A FIGHT
THAN TO START SWINGING.
(133)

TALK'S CHEAP. ACTIONS SPEAK.
THE THINGS WE DO WHEN NO ONE'S
LOOKING DEFINE US.
(132)

WE CONSOLE OURSELVES
WE'RE IN CONTROL: THE CAPTAIN.
NOPE! JUST PASSENGERS.
(130)

TOO MANY OF US
DON'T KNOW OUR OWN HEARTS, OR MINDS,
YET ACT LIKE WE DO.
(128)

WE DECEIVE OURSELVES
WHEN WE BLAME OTHERS, NOT US,
FOR *OUR* BAD CHOICES.
(127)

WHEN SEEKING ANSWERS
THE MOST CRUCIAL STEP IS TO
ASK THE RIGHT QUESTIONS.
(124)

DAYS OF FUTURE PAST.
TODAY BECOMES YESTERDAY
IF WE DON'T REFLECT.
(120)

IN ORDER TO FLY
GRAVITY MUST BE OVERCOME.
OPEN YOUR MIND. SOAR!
(119)

LIFE'S ONE CERTAINTY
IS DEATH. IN THE INTERIM,
IT'S OURS TO DEFINE.
(118)

OTHER'S OPINIONS
OFTEN GUIDE OUR BEHAVIOR.
WHY? WHO'S LIFE IS IT?
(117)

WITHOUT COMPASSION
AND EMPATHY WE CANNOT
UNDERSTAND OTHERS.
(116)

HUMAN VANITY
CREATES A UNIQUENESS MYTH
THAT WILL DESTROY US.
(115)

LOOK IN A MIRROR
LIKE WHAT YOU SEE? IF YES, GOOD.
IF NOT, GET TO WORK!
(114)

EXPECT GUARANTEES?
THINK LIFE IS PREDICTABLE?
WAKE UP! STOP DREAMING.
(113)

STAY INSIDE THE LINES
OR IGNORE THEM? WHICH WAY'S BEST?
WE'RE NOT ALL THE SAME.
(108)

WELCOME TO MY WORLD.
ONLY ONE RULE: ANYTHING GOES.
EAT – OR BE EATEN.
(107)

LETTING GO IS HARD.
BUT, TO MOVE FORWARD, WE'VE GOT
TO STOP LOOKING BACK.
(105)

HERE'S WHAT LIFE'S TAUGHT ME:
MOST PEOPLE PROTECT THEMSELVES –
WHATEVER IT TAKES.
(104)

LOCKED DEEP DOWN INSIDE,
DESPITE OUR MANY FACES,
WE ALL KNOW OUR TRUTHS.
(103)

DANCE WITH THE DEVIL?
HAVE FUN! ONE THING'S FOR CERTAIN:
PAY NOW – PAY LATER.
(102)

WHEN YOU'RE DIFFERENT
SOONER OR LATER PEOPLE
WILL DEMAND YOU CHANGE.
(101)

SAVE YOURSELF BEFORE
YOU TRY TO SAVE SOMEONE ELSE,
OR YOU'LL BOTH GO DOWN.
(99)

HERE'S AN ASSUMPTION
THAT WILL SURELY DO YOU HARM:
PEOPLE TELL THE TRUTH.
(96)

SURE, I'LL GET YOU OFF!
IT'S AN OPEN AND SHUT CASE.
THAT'LL BE CASH, UPFRONT.
(90)

RACE/BIGOTRY ARE,
FOR THOSE WITHOUT MONEY OR
POWER, EGO BOOSTS.
(88)

CURIOUS ABOUT
WHAT'S WHISPERED BEHIND YOUR BACK?
WHO ARE THEY TO JUDGE?
(87)

THERE'S NO BUYING BACK
ONCE WE HAVE CONSIGNED OUR SOUL.
EVIL HOARDS ITS WAGE.
(82)

PROGRESS IS MEASURED
IN INCHES, NOT MILES. SMALL STEPS …
PLANNED, UNWAVERING.
(80)

"AN EYE FOR AN EYE."
HOW DOES THIS RECONCILE WITH
"TURN THE OTHER CHEEK"?
(79)

THERE'S A PRICE ONE PAYS
FOR ALWAYS GETTING THEIR WAY:
SO SOON YOU'RE ALONE.
(78)

THE NEW GOLDEN RULE?
"DO UNTO OTHERS OR THEY'LL
DO IT TO YOU FIRST."
(77)

CORRECTING MISTAKES,
REBUILDING BURNT BRIDGES, MEANS
SHEDDING ALL PRETENSE.
(75)

SEEKING TO AMEND
A LIFE TIME OF WRONG CHOICES
REQUIRES RIGHT CHOICES.
(74)

JOUSTING WITH WIND MILLS?
SO? SOMEBODY SHOULD DO IT,
KEEPING HOPE ALIVE.
(73)

ALL MOANERS, WHINERS,
VICTIMS AND WHY--ME--LORD TYPES:
YOU MAKE YOUR OWN LUCK.
(69)

MAN'S ACCOMPLISHMENTS
PALE BESIDE OUR GREATEST SKILL:
KILLING EACH OTHER.
(65)

WE ALL RESIST CHANGE.
SAFETY FIRST, RIGHT? BUT: *"NOTHING
VENTURED, NOTHING GAINED."*
(62)

SEEING A PROBLEM
AND DOING NOTHING ONLY
MAKES IT WORSE. WHY WAIT?
(61)

YOU CAN'T HUG YOUR KIDS
EN0UGH. YOU CAN'T KISS YOUR SPOUSE
TOO MUCH. DO IT. NOW!
(59)

OPPORTUNITY
RARELY KNOCKS TWICE. WHEN IT DOES,
BEST OPEN THAT DOOR!
(45)

HOW CAN WE KNOW WHAT
WE'RE GOOD AT IF WE LACK THE
COURAGE TO FIND OUT?
(43)

LIFE'S NOT A PRECISE
SCIENCE: TRIAL -- ERROR -- LEARN FROM
YOUR MISTAKES. WISE UP!
(42)

RESPECT'S A TWO-WAY
STREET. YOU DON'T GET WHAT YOU WON'T
GIVE. LOOK BOTH WAYS!
(40)

THERE'S NEVER ONLY
ONE WAY. THOSE WHO THINK SO, CAUSE
MOST OF OUR PROBLEMS.
(38)

WE'RE ALL IN LOVE WITH
OUR DELUSIONS. THEY'RE COMFY,
AND, IN NO TIME, REAL.
(37)

CHANGE IS POSSIBLE,
NOT LIKELY. WE ARE HARD WIRED. WITH
LUCK, WE MIGHT EVOLVE.
(34)

IN THE DEPTHS OF OUR
SOUL, A TUG-OF-WAR RAGES:
LIGHT? OR DARK? WE CHOOSE!
(32)

PURE, TOTAL SILENCE,
MAY ONLY BE IMAGINED:
MIND WISPERS NON-STOP!
(30)

THE READY ANSWER
AS TO WHY WE DO MOST THINGS?
SELFISH GAINS; QUICK CASH!
(29)

WITH DEMOCRACY
GOING IN THE BOOTH'S A MUST.
NO VOTE, NO BITCHING!
(26)

WHEN GIVEN AN INCH,
MOST TAKE A MILE ... THEN BLAME YOU
IF SOMETHING GOES WRONG!
(25)

THOSE CELL PHONE VOYEURS
ARE RUNNING AMOK. WATCH OUT.
YOU'RE A PHOTO OP!
(24)

TRUTH'S HARD TO COME BY.
DON'T EXPECT IT FROM OTHERS.
BE YOUR OWN COUNSEL!
(23)

HOW MUCH DO WE CARE?
WHAT'S OUR EMPATHY QUOTIENT?
DEPENDS: "WHO IS IT?"
(22)

WHAT CAN WE COUNT ON?
NOT COUNTING ON THOSE WHO SAY
"YOU CAN COUNT ON ME!"
(21)

THERE'S RIGHT AND THERE'S WRONG.
TO SOME, RIGHT'S WRONG … OTHERS RIGHT.
IS THAT RIGHT OR WRONG?
(20)

THERE'S BAD AND THERE'S GOOD.
FOR SOME, BAD'S GOOD … OTHERS BAD.
IS THAT BAD OR GOOD?
(19)

FRESH FACED COLLEGE GRAD:
"NO, I NEVER WROTE A CHECK."
"WHAT'S A BANK BALANCE?"
(18)

LIFE'S A CRAPSHOOT.
HOW MUCH YOU WILLING TO RISK?
PLACE YOUR BETS. ROLL'EM!
(17)

C'MON, YOU KNOW ME!
I'M GOOD FOR IT, I PROMISE!!
THE CHECK'S IN THE MAIL!!!
(16)

HURRY UP! MOVE! GO!
NO TIME TO THINK ABOUT IT.
WHAT'S "IT" ANYWAY?
(15)

EVER WONDER WHY
THINGS NEVER GO YOUR WAY?
WE MAKE OUR OWN LUCK!
(14)

PRIDE PREDICTS THE FALL;
DEVOURING ITS OWNER WHOLE
RATHER THAN "GIVE IN!"
(13)

ATTRIBUTING BLAME
AWAY FROM OURSELVES ABSOLVES
AND SOOTHES OUR CONSCIENCE.
(6)

SO EASY TO SAY
SOMEONE ELSE'S WILL HELD SWAY:
THE COWARD'S SAFE PLAY.
(5)

BOOK TWO

COSMIC REFLECTIONS

LET ME GET THIS STRAIGHT:
YOU WANT ME TO WAIT BY HEAV-
EN'S GATE FOR *HOW* LONG?
(2115)

SOME HUMAN HES AND
SHES NEED TO BE NONE OF THESE.
IT'S "THEY" OR "WE", PLEASE.
(2110)

TEARS APPEAR TO CLEANSE
OUR SINS – NOT NEAR AS MANY
STILL DORMANT WITHIN.
(2105)

ON MY WAY TO HELL,
I PAUSED A SPELL TO SEE IF
I COULD TELL ME … HOW?
(2089)

"MY MIND SEES WHAT MY
SOUL FEELS. MY HEART SINGS THESE, MY
REALITIES. ME."
(2088)

THOSE TURGID SEAS OF
MEMORIES WILL SWAMP YOU OR
SPIT YOU CLEAR: DROWNED? FREED?
(2081)

I'LL CONSORT WITH ROGUES;
PANDER; BEGUILE – ALL THE WHILE
FORCING THEM TO SMILE.
(2074)

PRIDE'S PRICE? FROM PRECI-
PICE TO ABYSS, A SURE FALL
INTO HELL'S BLACK STALL.
(2070)

DEFLECTED LIGHT'S FAR OUT
OF FOCUS. LIFE LESSONS RE-
DIRECT ITS LOCUS.
(2066)

NIGHT'S OF FUTURE DAYS
CAST SHADOWS ON OUR PAST, SET-
TING NOW'S HOPE'S ABLAZE.
(2065)

EVER WISH YOU DIDN'T
KNOW WHAT YOU KNOW? LIFE MIGHT FLOW
EASIER – YOU KNOW?
(2061)

CAN YOU WRITE SOMETHING
IN SEVENTEEN SYLLABLES
THAT ENDS WITH *"KISS ME"*?
(2053)

WHEN CAUGHT WITH YOUR PANTS
DOWN, TURN IT AROUND: ZEN'EM! SMILE,
DON'T FROWN; WHO'LL GIVE IN?
(2052)

MANY SEE THE UNI-
VERSE AS A CELESTI-
AL HEARSE: HARD; COLD; TERSE.
(2047)

OLD ENOUGH TO HAVE
BEEN THERE, TOO YOUNG TO NOT CARE:
BETWEEN HOPE AND DARE.
(2042)

IN THE BLINK OF AN
EYE, WE'RE HERE, DONE, GONE. THE U-
NIVERSE LIGHT SPEEDS ON.
(2039)

SATAN'S SPAWN COULD BE
ANY PAWN WHOSE EGO WHISPERS
"ONLY I CAN KNOW."
(2035)

MAN'S CLIMB STALLS WHEN HE
SPIRALS THROUGH JOYOUS *"WE"*, TO
CACOPHONOUS *"ME."*
(2033)

THE WAYS OF MEN HAVEN'T
CHANGED SINCE THE DAY THEY DID BE-
GIN. MEANS? YES. SAME ENDS.
(2029)

APROPOS OF CHA-
OS, I TOSS THIS TO THE WIND:
LET THE GAMES BEGIN!
(2027)

THE DARK OF NIGHT'S SMIR-
KING DELIGHT IS MAN'S ABID-
ING, BROODING FRIGHT.
(2026)

WHAT I SEE ISN'T WHAT
YOU SEE … PROBABLY. YOUR BRAIN
TELLS YOU, MINE ME. SEE?
(2025)

INTUITION IN-
FORMS INTELLECT IN IDI-
OSYNCRATIC ID.
(2023)

WE'D BE DERELICT
NOT TO INFLICT PUNISHMENT
ON YOU … IT'S LONG DUE!
(2014)

HEARD THIS REFRAIN: *"RIGHT*
AS RAIN"? WELL, HERE'S ITS COUSIN:
"NO PAIN, NO GAIN." MOVE!
(2010)

BETTER DEMONS WITH-
IN, THAN THOSE WITHOUT. AT LEAST
THEY'RE YOUR KISSIN' KIN.
(2007)

THE RIGHTS WE DO, DON'T
RIGHT THE WRONGS WE CHOOSE. PRAY THEY'RE
EVEN WHEN YOU'RE THROUGH.
(1999)

CONSIGNED TO PURGA-
TORY, RESIGNED TO DAMNA-
TION, *I'LL* FIND A WAY OUT.
(1997)

WHO I WAS, ISN'T *WHO*
I AM. WHO I AM, ISN'T *WHO*
I'LL BE. SOON. NEW ... *ME?*
(1995)

ATTITUDES CAN BE
ADJUSTED, WHEN THEIR OWNERS AREN'T
ENRAGED OR ENCRUSTED.
(1994)

ME? HEART – PETER PAN;
MIND? -- METHUSALAH. RECON-
CILE THIS ... IF YOU CAN.
(1982)

OPTIONS, REDUCED AS
YEARS FLY BY, SOON BECOME JUST
ONE: WHEN WILL WE DIE?
(1977)

MESMERIZED BY LONE-
LINESS, WE EMBRACE IT'S SELF-
PROTECTIVE CARESS.
(1976)

THE MORE I KNOW, THE
THE LESS I REMEMBER. WONDER
WHEN I'LL KNOW ZERO?
(1974)

LORD, LET ME LEAVE WITH
A TWINKLE IN MY EYE AND
LAUGHTER IN MY HEART.
(1973)

IF YOU USE YOU AS
YOUR LENS ON REALITY
YOU'LL NEVER SEE US.
(1971)

BEFORE I GO, PLEASE,
HELP ME TO SEE WHY MOST CHOOSE
"A SHOW" V. "TO KNOW."
(1965)

TO SURVIVE, WE MUST
FOCUS ON THE MUNDANE, OUR
LIVES, MAINLY, INANE.
(1961)

CERTITUDE, LIKE REC-
TITUDE, REQUIRES EITHER DE-
MENTIA OR QUALUDES.
(1957)

HEAVEN KNOWS THAT HELL
KNOWS. HELL'S THE SAME. SO ...WHAT'S THE
REASON FOR THEIR GAMES?
(1956)

DOES THE BEGINNING
OF OUR END BEGIN AT BIRTH?
BEFORE? AFTER? WHEN?
(1949)

WHEN HOPE DIES, LIFE PET-
RIFIES. YOU MIGHT SURVIVE, BUT
YOUR SOUL'S NOT ALIVE.
(1946)

BREVITY AND LEV-
ITY LET SPEECH BE DISMEM-
BERED AND REMEMBERED.
(1936)

TIME'S ITS OWN KEEPER.
NO ONE ESCAPES ITS CONSTRAINTS:
MAN'S TRUE GRIM REAPER.
(1935)

THOSE TIMES WHEN FEELINGS
GET IN THE WAY OF SENSE, HELP
US TO SHED PRETENSE.
(1930)

PERFECTION (CONTROL):
A REFLECTION OF EGO'S
FEAR OF REJECTION.
(1923)

"CRAZY" ASSUMES SHARED
NORMS OF RATIONALITY.
DO YOU KNOW ANY?
(1921)

WE'VE GOT NINE OVER
THAT LINE. ONE TO GO 'TIL END
OF SHOW. WHO CARES, BRO?
(1906)

TO FEEL IS TO IN-
VITE PAIN. AND, LET'S BE HONEST,
WHAT'S TO GAIN ... MORE PAIN?
(1904)

PERPLEXED BY MAN'S BE-
HAVIOR? PAUSE. REFLECT: WE CRU-
CIFIED OUR *'SAVIOR'*.
(1897)

DELUSION REIGNS; CON-
FUSION IS QUEEN; SANITY'S
FLEEING ON THE SCREEN.
(1893)

CONTINUOUS, COUN-
TERINTUITIVE CHALLEN-
GES CREATE CHAOS.
(1892)

THE ONLY TRADI-
TION I'M BOUND TO IS BREATHING –
IT'S AN ADDICTION.
(1888)

THE SPECIOUS INTENT
OF ADVERTISEMENT IS TO
GET YOUR SPECIE SPENT!
(1882)

WHY BE COURTEOUS,
WHEN OUTRAGEOUS IS SO MUCH
MORE EFFICACIOUS?
(1881)

A POX ON MAKING
SENSE. LOGIC'S TOO INTENSE. LET
FEELINGS' REIGN COMMENCE!
(1877)

BEAUTY'S PERSONAL;
INTELLIGENCE UNIVER-
SAL; PRETTY SMART, SEE?
(1875)

AS LONG AS I AM E-
LUSIVE, NOTHING CAN BE CON-
CLUSIVE. SO, I HIDE.
(1859)

THE END WON'T BE LIKE
WE'D PREDICT: DOOM, GLOOM, CHAOS.
NOPE. WORSE – WE'LL END US.
(1853)

LOSS OF FACE: EGO'S
CONTUSION. WHY ONE WOULD CARE
IS *THEIR* CONFUSION.
(1852)

GODS. DEVILS. EACH WOO
WITH BARNUM-THEMED CLAIMS IN
ETERNITY'S GAME.
(1842)

IN BLACK, DARKEST NIGHT,
WHAT'S YOUR TORMENT? YOUR DELIGHT?
WHICH BRINGS FRIGHT? WHICH LIGHT?
(1835)

TALKIN' TIME'S EXPIRED.
AIN'T NO COMPROMISE DESIRED.
NOW? GUNS WILL BE FIRED.
(1830)

WHAT'S BEST, ME BEING
ME OR THE PERSON THAT MY
FRIENDS SAY I SHOULD BE?
(1812)

WHAT ARE YOU MADE OF?
IF PUSH COMES TO SHOVE, WILL YOU
CHOOSE MONEY – OR LOVE?
(1810)

WHO KNOW'S IF LIVING
LIFE'S TOUGHER THAN LEAVING? WHAT
ODDS ARE THEY GIVING?
(1808)

IS LIFE A CONTIN-
UANCE; PURPOSEFUL PROGRES-
SION; OR CIRCUMSTANCE?
(1804)

SIMPLICITY GUAR-
ANTEES LESS ANXIETY,
MORE HAPPY. LET GO.
(1803)

CLOSE YOUR EYES. TRY TO
VISUALIZE LIFE WITHOUT
YOU. TOO SOON IT'S TRUE.
(1794)

WHAT DOES IT SAY WHEN
GROWN-UPS REFUSE TO PLAY UN-
LESS THEY GET THEIR WAY?
(1792)

ENDINGS, INHERENT
TO BEGINNINGS, AREN'T APPAR-
ENT, BUT ADHERENT.
(1782)

BETWEEN RIGHT AND WRONG
A SYREN'S SONG LURES THE WEAK
AND BEGUILES THE STRONG.
(1775)

CRIME: TOO HAPPY. TRIED,
CONVICTED, SENTENCED: (I'M TO SEE
ONLY NEWS T.V.).
(1773)

AGAIN, LOST TO US
IS: ABSENT COMPROMISE, WE
REVERT TO CHAOS.
(1770)

TIRED OF PLAYERS PLAY-
ING YOU, THEN SAYING YOU'RE TO
BLAME? WHY? THAT'S LIFE'S GAME!
(1768)

GRAY ONE, SAY YOUR TRUE
AS IT COMES TO YOU. RECALL –
RECKONING'S SOON DUE.
(1766)

WITH NO HOPE OF EX-
EMPTION, I'M FINESSING A
REDEMPTION OPTION.
(1764)

WHAT WOULD ONE PAY TO
BE ABLE TO SAY *"I DID
IT MY WAY"* – AND DID!
(1758)

WE CELEBRATE CHA-
OS AND REVEL IN HATE. WE'RE
ALL LOST. AIN'T IT GREAT?
(1757)

MISTY PURPLE HAZE
TINTS A DAWNING SUN'S PINKISH
RAYS. WAKE SLEEPY DAY.
(1756)

CHIAROSCURO
HAUNTINGLY TINTS CHILLING HINTS
OF MENDACITY.
(1755)

RESTLESS BRAIN PONDERS
RANDOM CHAOS: THEN, NOW, BEST,
WORST, ALL. I WANDER.
(1745)

WHAT IS, WAS AND WILL
BE, AGAIN. MAN FORGETS, THEN
MUST RE-LEARN ... 'TIL WHEN?
(1718)

DREADED GHOULS BE WE WHO
DARE NOT SEE THE MISERY
WE INFLICT DAILY.
(1715)

IF'S LIVING'S BREATHING,
I'M DOING THAT. IF THERE'S MORE,
PLEASE! WHAT IS IT? STAT!
(1698)

I DON'T KNOW HOW I
KNOW. WISH I DIDN'T. BUT, SINCE I
DO, IT'S TIME TO GO.
(1695)

FACTS, BORING, BITING, DIG
IN. WHY LISTEN? IGNORE THEM!
IT'S EASY. LIES WIN.
(1693)

"TRUTH" RIDES THE TIDES. IT
EBBS AND FLOWS WITH TIME AS GEN-
ERATIONS DECIDE.
(1692)

PLEASE LORD, WHY IS THERE
NO JUSTICE, ONLY THE VER-
DICT ONE CAN AFFORD?
(1691)

SUN'S HIDDEN. SKY'S GRAY.
QUITE UNBIDDEN, A RAINBOW
BRIGHTENS THE DAY. CALM.
(1688)

I ALWAYS THOUGHT I
WAS TOUGH. I'M CALLING MY BLUFF –
GOT SOME HEAVY STUFF.
(1686)

NO MORE CIVILIZED
THAN NEANDERTHALS, WE LIVE
LARGER LIES ... THAT'S ALL.
(1681)

FUNCTION DICTATES FORM –
EXCEPT FOR HUMANS, WHOOSE FORM
DETERMINES FUNCTION.
(1673)

I'VE NO FUTURE. JUST
A PAST. WHO KNEW IT'D GO BY
SO FAST? MY DIE'S CAST!
(1667)

INTUITION ISN'T
INTELLECTUAL. IT'S IN-
STINCT INITIATED.
(1658)

IN MY YOUTH THE THINGS
I'D DO! THE COURSES I FLEW! FADED,
GRAY, WERE THEY TRUE?
(1655)

I USED TO WONDER …
WHY? NOW, I WONDER WHY
I EVER WONDERED WHY.
(1640)

SHOULD: PSYCHOLOGY;
COULD: PERSONALITY; WOULD:
YOUR PHILOSOPHY.
(1638)

I'VE LOST ALL IDEN-
TITY; I'M BECOME A NON-
ENTITY. I'M FREE!
(1633)

BORN OF CALAMI-
TY, RAISED IN UNCERTAINTY,
WONDER WHO I'LL BE?
(1629)

HOW MANY RUE THE
DARK DEEDS THEY DO, IF ANY?
AT BEST, IT'S TOO FEW.
(1613)

YOU SHOULD HAVE KNOWN
YOUR COVER WOULD BE BLOWN. EGO
WOULDN'T LET YOU LET GO.
(1611)

MEMORIES, POUROUS, RETAIN
WHAT WE DEEM BEST FOR
US. THE REST? BOGUS.
(1603)

PROXIMITY'S LI-
ABILITY; DISTANCE DE-
NIABILITY.
(1587)

THIS WORLD SPINS. TIME WHIRLS.
MANKIND PLAYS THE SAME GAMES, WHICH
NONE CAN EVER WIN.
(1582)

WHAT WILL BE, NO ONE
CAN SEE, BUT -- HISTORY IS
MANKIND'S WARRANTY.
(1577)

IF WE DON'T MEND OUR
WAYS SOON, EARTH WILL BE LIKE A
FULL, FILTHY SPITTOON.
(1574)

WEARY OF BEING,
LEERY OF SEEING ALL THAT
HAS BEEN, BE AGAIN.
(1570)

THE MUSIC OF THE
SPHERES PLAYS IN ALL EARS, BUT EACH
HEARS A UNIQUE TUNE.
(1561)

PART OF ME WANTS TO
STAY, PART TO FLEE. MAN'S WORLD IN-
CREASINGLY HAUNTS ME.
(1556)

INDIVIDUAL
IDENTITY IS INSID-
IOUS ILLUSION.
(1555)

AT BEST AMBIGU-
OUS, NEVERTHELESS, I CAN
ATTEST TO BEING.
(1554)

THE HEART HIDES SECRETS
THE MIND HASN'T DISCOVERED -- YET.
IT WILL. WITH REGRETS.
(1551)

TOO MANY PONDER
WHAT-IF, MAYBE; IGNORING
TRUE REALITY.
(1545)

CONFUSION, FEAR DIS-
APPEAR WHEN THIS BECOMES CLEAR:
TRUTH'S AN ILLUSION.
(1543)

TIME TICKS ON. WE'RE HERE,
SOON GONE. THOSE WHO PROCEED WON'T
HEED. WHY? TIME TICKS ON.
(1542)

ISOLATION IN-
VITES IMAGINATION, IN-
TENSIFYING "I."
(1531)

THERE'S NO WAY TO KNOW
WHEN YOU'LL GO, SO … DO WHAT YOU
MUST. JUST LEAVE NO RUST.
(1529)

SEDUCED BY YOUR AL-
LURE, UNDER PRESSURE, I SUC-
CUMBED: ABJECT FAILURE.
(1517)

PONDERING WHAT-IFS
CAUSES MENTAL RIFTS. THE MIND SHIFTS
GEARS: FAST-SLOW-WANDERING.
(1511)

I SEE THE LIGHT ... IT
ISN'T RIGHT – FLICKERING, UNSTEAD-
Y. I'M NOT READY.
(1509)

THAT FINE LINE BETWEEN
ACCEPTABLE AND NOT VARIES. IT'S
TAUGHT; NEVER TAUT.
(1499)

SEE IF YOU AGREE:
APT AGING METAPHOR? *TIN MAN
WITH AN OIL CAN."*
(1491)

TIME'S FOOL, I LET IT
SLIP AWAY BY IGNORING
LIFE'S RULE: SEIZE EACH DAY!
(1484)

WHAT'S THE CORRELA-
TION BETWEEN INSANITY
AND HOPE? CLEAR TO ME.
(1483)

I'M IN AND OUT. NOT
LOSIN' IT YET ... BUT, CERTAIN-
LY CONFUSIN' IT.
(1475)

A NO BOUNDRY
NON-LINEARITY IS
ESSENTIAL TO ME.
(1474)

MANY OF US TRY
OUR BEST TO SABOTAGE OUR
OWN SELF-INTEREST.
(1470)

THAT HOLE IN YOUR HEART
WON'T HEAL UNTIL YOU START TO
FEEL YOU ARE WORTH IT.
(1468)

THOSE THINGS WE DON'T DO
OR INTEND TO, BUT PASS, COULD'VE
BEEN A WHOLE NEW YOU.
(1467)

CRAZY! WHAT ARE THE
ODDS THAT I WOULD TAKE A CHANCE
ON TAKING A CHANCE?
(1466)

ROILING WAVES OF E-
MOTIONS INUNDATE LOGIC'S
FALSE CALMING NOTIONS.
(1464)

TIME'S PUPPET- STRINGS SUS-
PEND US ALL. NO ONE'S IMMUNE:
WE DANCE TO ITS TUNE.
(1463)

ROUND-AND-ROUND IT GOES.
ONE MORE DAY OF MAN'S WOES. CAN
WE CHANGE? OUR PAST SHOWS.
(1462)

"PEACE ON EARTH?" IMPOSS-
IBLE. *"GOOD WILL TO MEN?"* IM-
PROBABLE. *"JOY?"* – BULL …
(1457)

I'VE SEEN THE STUFF MOST
ARE MADE OF. THERE'S GOOD, BAD AND
BEST – BUT, NOT MUCH LOVE.
(1442)

IS THERE SUCH A THING
AS TOO MUCH OF A GOOD THING?
-- CAN'T HAVE ENOUGH GOOD.
(1440)

THE PART OF *"I"* THAT
SHARES *"WE"* IS HOW ITS SUPPOSED
TO BE. NOT *"ME-ME."*
(1435)

MAN'S BEST DISGUISE IS
"CIVILIZED" – OUR ALIBI
TO CHEAT, STEAL, TELL LIES.
(1429)

I DON'T KNOW WHAT I
DON'T. I DO KNOW WHAT I DO.
SO -- DO I OR DON'T?
(1428)

WE ALL SHOULD SEE THE
IMPORTANCE OF SIMPLICI-
TY. MOST DON'T ... SADLY.
(1425)

I CAN'T EXPLAIN MY
MANY FAUX PAS. THEY EXPLAIN
THE JABS TO MY JAW.
(1424)

FAILURE'S INHERENT
FOR SUCCESS. GOT TO KNOW WHAT
DOESN'T WORK THEN PROGRESS.
(1423)

WHY ISN'T THE FIRTH OF
FOURTH A FIRST OR FIFTH? WHAT IS
A FIRTH? WHAT'S IT WORTH?
(1421)

HAD I NOT BEEN A
PRETENDER, I COULD HAVE BEEN
A CONTENDER ... SAD.
(1420)

CLOUDS OF OMINOUS
PORTENT CIRCUMVENT MY IN-
TENT: CAN'T TAKE A HINT.
(1418)

SEEDS OF DOUBT WILL SPROUT
WHEN NURTURED BY PAIN AND SHAME.
ITS NAME? – CONTROL GAME.
(1417)

RARE A PAIR THAT CARE
ENOUGH TO STAY THE COURSE. DARE
TRY? TOO HARD ... DIVORCE!
(1415)

THAT GRIM REAPER'S A
KEEPER. NO ONE ESCAPES HIS
NOOSE. ALL TRY. ALL LOSE.
(1414)

IN DARKS OF DAY, AND
LIGHTS OF NIGHT, SHADOWS PLAY WHERE
I CAN HIDE – AWAY.
(1406)

IS MY DESIRE FOR
DESIRE MUCH, MUCH HIGHER THAN
I DARE ASPIRE?
(1399)

YE WHO WOULD BE EN-
LIGHTENED, PREPARE THYSELVES WELL,
LEST YE BE FRIGHTENED.
(1398)

WE SHOULDN'T FIGHT EACH
BATTLE TO WIN. SOMETIMES THE
MAIN THING'S TO JOIN IN.
(1386)

ANSWER ME THIS: WHY
IS MAN HERE – TO SEEK ETER-
NAL BLISS, OR DRINK BEER?
(1384)

SAGES SIGH, *"FOLLOW
YOUR HEART."* MY REPLY: IF I
DO, I'LL FALL APART.
(1379)

SOMEDAY, SOMEHOW, I'LL
SEE A WAY TO MAKE YOU THINK
OF ME AND SAY *"WOW!"*
(1378)

EMPATHY WANES. DE-
CENCY DIES. SOCIETY
FEIGNS SURPRISE. GOD CRIES.
(1376)

ARE MEMORIES FIXED
VIEWS OR EVOLVING UPDATES
OF OUR BRAIN'S FALSE NEWS?
(1355)

WHO WILL I BE TO-
DAY, THE SAME OLD ME OR STAR
IN A BRAND-NEW PLAY?
(1345)

I GET SNAPSHOTS OF
WHO I'D LIKE TO BE THEY'RE
NOT CLEAR: CLOUDY, MISTY.
(1325)

BETWEEN ILLUSION'S
CERTAINTY AND DELUSION'S
FANTASY, WHO'S ME?
(1323)

NO ONE'S INNOCENT.
THOUGHT, WORD OR DEED IS SUF-
FICIENT PROOF OF INTENT.
(1313)

SIMPLE IS AS SIM-
PLE DOES. COMPLEXITY CON-
FUSES WHAT IT WAS.
(1310)

THOSE WHICH I GET RIGHT
BARELY MATCH WRONG. THIS FIGHT
WILL NOT EASE LIFE-LONG.
(1309)

SYNERGY HAS DIED.
CRY! SOCIETY'S GLUE IS
CRACKED, DRIED. SIGH GOOD-BYE.
(1308)

TO THE DEGREE I
AGREE WITH YOUR THEORY
LET ME SAY, *"WE'LL SEE."*
(1306)

PERCEPTION'S NARROW
AS BIASES GROW. BLOCKING
LIGHT INVITES THE NIGHT.
(1303)

ERE OUR RETURN TO
DUST, WE MUST LEARN THIS: WOE DOTH
BEFALL ALL WHO TRUST.
(1301)

A BLESSING AND CURSE?
I SEE THE BIG PICTURE, YET
DETAILS ARE MY HEARSE.
(1297)

EMPATHY IS ON
THE BRINK, SADLY, BECAUSE MOR-
ALITY'S EXTINCT.
(1296)

VIEWING MAN'S PRESENT
STAGE FROM A GILDED CAGE, HOT TEARS
COOL MY BURNING RAGE.
(1292)

COMES THE DAY OF DE-
CIDING, YOU'LL BE SORTED. DOUBT NOT:
THERE'LL BE NO HIDING.
(1286)

CONTRARY TO COM-
PREHENSION, YOU OCCUPY
ONE DIMENSION: SELF.
(1281)

MANKIND'S NIMBLE MIND'S
BLIND TO THE NARROW CONFINES
OF IT'S SELF-DESIGN.
(1276)

SILENCE IS SOUND. LOST'S
FOUND. SLEEP'S AWAKE. GIVE TO TAKE.
YOU ARE I. TRUTHS LIE.
(1275)

HOLD ME. CONSOLE ME.
HELP ME BECOME WHOLE. A BLACK
HOLE'S HOLLOWED MY SOUL.
(1268)

I HAVE SEEN THE LIGHT.
IT'S SCARY! I'M UPTIGHT, CON-
TRARY. SO ... HELP! RIGHT?
(1246)

A COMMUNITY
OF ONE, I GRANT IMMUNI-
TY FROM ALL I'VE DONE.
(1244)

PORTIONS OF MY LIFE
WERE PRE-RECORDED. ELSE HOW DID
IT GET SO CONTORTED?
(1243)

WE ARE WHO WE WERE
AND WILL BE. MANKIND'S NATURE
DOESN'T VARY -- PITY.
(1240)

CLOSE? IN SPACE A MIL-
LION MILES. IN A HORSE RACE, BY
A NOSE. SO, ... WHO KNOWS?
(1236)

OUR QUEST FOR RELE-
VANCE IS AT ODDS WITH NATURE'S
COLD AMBIVALENCE.
(1230)

TIME – HOW QUICKLY IT
DOTH FLY! – IS NOT, NOR ERE WILL
BE, OUR KIND'S ALLY.
(1224)

GRANT ME CLARITY:
INSIGHT INTO MAN'S HABIT
OF CALAMITY.
(1223)

DAYS. NIGHTS. ALONE. THOUGHTS
STRANGE, LOCO. PONDERING UN-
KNOWNS: WHEN, IF, I'LL KNOW.
(1219)

SO. THINK YOU'RE SECURE?
WRONG! KNOW THIS FOR SURE: TO MOST
YOU AIN'T WORTH A SONG.
(1218)

PARTS OF MY HEART ARE
SCATTERED ALONG THE PATHS OF
MY PAST: I'M SHATTERED.
(1213)

THERE ARE A FEW WHO
WILL SAY OR DO ANYTHING
TO GET THEIR WAY. YOU?
(1212)

IT ISN'T ACQUIRING,
BUT DESIRING AND ASPIR-
ING, THAT INSPIRE DREAMS.
(1200)

PERPLEXED DEFINES OUR
KIND. IT'S NOT MAN'S NATURE TO
REFINE PEACE OF MIND.
(1194)

HOW DO WE KNOW WHEN
IT'S TIME TO LET GO? FEELINGS?
WORDS? MY HEART'S REELING.
(1188)

TOOK THE CHANCE. NEVER
THOUGHT I WOULD – LOVE; ROMANCE. NONE
OF IT'S EVER GOOD.
(1186)

THEY SAY ONE GETS FROM
LIFE, WHAT THEY PUT IN. WHEN DOES
THE GETTIN' BEGIN?
(1183)

YOU'RE NOT SAFE WHEN YOU'RE
NOT FREE. YOU'RE NOT FREE WHEN YOU'RE
NOT SAFE. BOTH OR – FLEE?
(1179)

MOURNING MEMORY'S
STEADY DEMISE, MY MIND MISTS,
AS TEARS FLOOD MY EYES.
(1177)

WATCHING HOW YOU ACT,
DEVOID OF GRACE AND TACT, I
THUS REACT: "F—K OFF!"
(1176)

I AM WHO I WILL
I AM. JUDGE ME NOT BY MY
GAME PLANS. THAT'S ALL SCAM.
(1174)

MOST OF US WHO HIDE
WISH WE WEREN'T SO IMPEDED ... IF
ONLY WE WERE NEEDED.
(1173)

SUGGESTED, NOT SHOWN. HINTED,
NOT KNOWN. SUBTLETY ATTRACTS
SUBLIMINALLY.
(1172)

MY MAIN GAME ISN'T FAME
OR GLORY, JUST A HAPPY
END TO LIFE'S STORY.
(1171)

IF I WERE HONEST,
I'D ADMIT I MADE A MESS
OF IT ... BEST TO FIB.
(1169)

REVERTING TO FORM'S
THE NORM. FEW ACT ON NEW-LEARNED
FACTS AFTER *"I SEE!"*
(1165)

MADLY, YOUR LONG SUP-
PRESSED MEMORY GNAWS AT THE
CORE OF MY PSYCHE.
(1163)

THE END'S NIGH, THOUGH NOT
FROM *"ON HIGH."* HUMANS WILL DE-
VISE THEIR OWN DEMISE.
(1156)

I SWEAR THERE'S TIMES WHEN
LIFE'S NOT FAIR. SEEMS LIKE CALAM-
ITY CHASES ME.
(1154)

LOGIC'S CALM A-TO-
Z IS SWAMPED BY EMOTION'S
TSUNAMI": *"ME" – "ME!"*
(1151)

I AM A COUNTRY
OF ONE, A CITIZEN OF
NONE. MY COUNT'S BEGUN.
(1148)

TELL ME QUICK: WHAT'S REAL?
WHAT WE SEE, THINK, FEEL OR WHAT
WERE'RE TOLD IS IDEAL?
(1147)

MINE'S THE LUCK OF ONE
WHO WON A MILLION BUCKS, THEN
GOT SMASHED BY A TRUCK.
(1144)

THAT LIFE'S CONFUSING
WE KNOW. WHY DO WE COMPOUND
THESE WOES WITH EGOS?
(1142)

WHEN WRONG ENDS DOES RIGHT
BEGIN OR ARE THESE IN SEP-
ARATE DIMENSIONS?
(1140)

I PONDER REAL-
ITY. I WONDER MYSTER-
Y ... LOCKED IN MY CAGE.
(1139)

PESSIMISTS SEE DARK,
OPTIMISTS LIGHT. REALISTS
KNOW DAY BECOMES NIGHT.
(1138)

I'VE COME TO THE CON-
CLUSION THAT I'M AN ILLU-
SION. NO ONE SEES ME.
(1137)

WE SHOULD KNOW RIGHT FROM
WRONG. THAT PART OF OUR BRAIN'S BEEN
MISSING FOR HOW LONG?
(1135)

PRETENSE GET THEE HENCE!
RELINQUISH THY CONTROL O'ER
MY SOUL. LEAVE ME WHOLE.
(1132)

IT'S AS PLATO SAID:
*"ONLY THE DEAD SEE THE END
OF WAR."* ... *"EVERMORE."*
(1130)

TOO MANY FAILS, TOO
FEW WINS. NOT SURE IF I CAN
FILL MY SAILS AGAIN.
(1126)

WHEN I'M DONE, IF THERE
COULD JUST BE ONE TO HOLD MY
HAND, TO UNDERSTAND ...
(1120)

A WHISPERING WIND
WINDS ITS WAY WISTFULLY,
WRAPPING ME IN WONDER.
(1096)

THE GAMES PEOPLE PLAY,
THE THINGS THAT THEY SAY: NOTHING'S
CHANGED SINCE MAN'S FIRST DAY.
(1093)

AS THE MIND GOES, SO
ALSO, THE SOUL? WHICH IS IN
CONTROL? CAN WE KNOW?
(1092)

I'M NOT IN THIS WORLD,
NOR ABOVE IT, BUT PARAL-
LEL, AT TIMES TANGENT.
(1089)

TOOK A WHILE, NOW I
SEE: CAN'T BLAME ANYONE, BUT
ME, FOR BEING ME.
(1088)

WE ARE NOT, "... IN-
DIVISIBLE WITH LIBERTY
AND JUSTICE FOR ALL."
(1082)

YOU GET WHAT YOU GIVE –
TRUE? WHAT IF THE ONE YOU GIVE
TO HASN'T A CLUE?
(1081)

SOLITUDE'S MY AT-
TITUDE: THE PRICE I PAY FOR
KEEPING PAIN AT BAY.
(1067)

FAITH IS BLIND. HOPE CAN
BE CRUEL. STILL, DAY IN, DAY OUT,
I'LL PLAY CUPID'S FOOL.
(1066)

PASSIONS AND EMO-
TIONS ROUSE GREAT UNREST IN THOSE
COLD SOULS NOT THUS BLESSED.
(1065)

ALWAYS ALONE, DEAD
SILENCE SCREAMS SHRILL WHISPERS OF
DREAD. NO CURSE IS WORSE.
(1064)

BEEN TO HELL, ROUND TRIP,
STARED DOWN THE ABYSS. THAT BELL
TOLLS *"NO MORE OF THIS."*
(1063)

THE PRICE OF KEEPING
AN OPEN MIND IS YOU'LL HAVE
A ONE OF A KIND.
(1061)

REASON DIED SOME TIME
AGO. THAT'S O.K. IT RARELY
WORKED ANYWAY.
(1059)

I PAID FOR MY KID'S
DEGREES THEN SAID *"PLEASE FEEL FREE
TO ROAM."* THEY MOVED HOME.
(1054)

I WENT ASTRAY – TOOK
THE EASY WAY. DON'T KNOW HOW
TO GET BACK ON TRACK.
(1049)

HISTORY'S MYSTER-
IES SOLVED: WHAT THE WINNERS DIDN'T
KNOW OR WANT KNOWN. CLEAR?
(1048)

GODS, INVENTED TO DIF-
FUSE FEAR, ASCENDED TO THEIR TRUE
ROLE: SOCIAL CONTROL.
(1041)

MORNING YEARS LONG PAST,
TWIGHLIGHT DAYS BEGUN, FEARS OF
AGEING DONE ... I WAIT.
(1034)

NONE CAN KNOW ABOUT
TOMORROW, SO NONE SHOULD LET
A DAY WASTE AWAY.
(1018)

IF WE ALL DRANK THE
SAME COOL-AID, AT THE SAME TIME,
WHAT WOULD HAPPEN NEXT?
(1017)

TIME'S SANDS DRIFT SLOWLY,
SURELY, FORWARD. WOULD THAT WE
COULD KNOW WHAT TOWARD.
(1016)

YOU'RE TOO GOOD AT WHAT
YOU DO. BET YOU THOUGHT NO ONE
WOULD CATCH ON TO YOU.
(1010)

MANKIND IS NOW AS
ALWAYS BEFORE: WE WHO WANT
PEACE, PREPARE FOR WAR.
(1009)

PINK, PURPLE, ORANGE:
TWILIGHT'S DISTINCT HUES. BEAUTY
NO ONE MISCONSTRUES.
(992)

MINUS A MIDDLE
EXTREMES COLLAPSE FROM THEIR OWN
DEAD WEIGHT. THUS: MAN'S FATE?
(972)

I HAD IT ALL, EX-
CEPT YOU. THEN I GOT THAT, TOO.
NOW WHAT DO I DO?
(970)

DO WE *"SEE"* WITH OUR
EYES OR DOES THE MIND *"DIRECT"*
WITH SUBTLE DISGUISE?
(967)

TRUST DIRT AND DUST. BE-
WARE CLEAN (PLAUSIBLE SUBTER-
FUGE FOR MEANS UNSEEN).
(964)

HAZY, SIMMERING
MID-DAY HEAT. NOTHING AS IT
SEEMS ... SIESTA DREAMS.
(933)

HANG YOUR HEADS! FIND A
PLACE TO HIDE. THAT DAY'S ARRIVED:
MORALITY DIED.
(932)

THERE'S A GOOD CHANCE LIFE'S
A DICE ROLL. IF NOT, THE GAME'S
RIGGED. WHO'S IN CONTROL?
(930)

THE CLOSER WE GET
TO ETERNITY THE FUR-
THER WE WANT TO BE.
(924)

AGED, A BODY AILS.
STILL, THE MIND MAINTAINS ITS GRACE
WHILE OUR WILL PREVAILS.
(917)

BEING ALONE EX-
ACTS A TOLL: IT REAMS A BLACK
HOLE IN YOUR SOUL.
(907)

HUMANITY WITH-
OUT INTEGRITY BECOMES
BESTIALITY.
(904)

LIFE HAPPENS. THERE'S NO
ORDER OR PLAN. WE MUST MAKE
THE MOST SENSE WE CAN.
(901)

EXPLAIN THIS, PLEASE: WHY,
WHEN GIVEN THE CHOICE, MOST IG-
NORE THEIR INNER VOICE?
(900)

TIME'S OUR MOST PRECIOUS
GIFT: WHO WE GIVE IT TO, GET
IT FROM, SHARE IT WITH.
(891)

MERCY'S A HUMAN
CONSTRUCT. ITS PURPOSE IS CLEAR:
BIRTH HOPE – ALLAY FEAR.
(884)

WORN, BLANK EYED, THEY SLIP
IN, THEN FADE AWAY, UNSEEN
BY MOST. WHAT'S THAT SAY?
(883)

THE PAST IS ALWAYS
PRESENT. THE PRESENT NEVER
PASSES. NEW IS OLD.
(875)

WE SEE WHAT OUR MIND
DIRECTS. THAT'S NOT SANE! IS
LIFE JUST SPECIAL EFFECTS?
(871)

ADMIT IT! YOUR WORST
FEAR IS THAT YOU REALLY ARE
WHO YOU THINK YOU ARE.
(864)

IF WE DON'T KNOW WHAT
WE DON'T KNOW, HOW CAN WE KNOW
WE DON'T KNOW SOMETHING?
(856)

AGED, LONELY, EACH DAY
ANTIPATHY'S SIREN SONG
SINGS CLEARER, NEARER.
(855)

ONLY FAITH'S INTERNAL
CONVICTION COUNTS, NOT
IT'S EXTERNAL EXPRESSION.
(852)

ONE'S TRUE MEASURE IS
THEIR DEPTH OF EMPATHY AND
BREDTH OF COMPASSION.
(851)

THAT'S ABSURD! WHAT I
SAID, ISN'T WHAT YOU HEARD. THERE'S LOOSE
GEARS IN YOUR HEAD.
(848)

IS WHO YOU SOUGHT TO
BE, WHO YOU OUGHT TO BE, OR
GOT CAUGHT UP BEING?
(845)

"HERE TODAY GONE TO-
MORROW." LAUGH WHILE YOU MAY. LOTS
OF TIME FOR SORROW.
(843)

MUCH MORE THAN I OUGHT
I'M OVERWROUGHT. NOT GUILT, JUST
FEAR OF BEING CAUGHT.
(840)

THANKS FOR SETTING THE
PACE. YOU GIVE US A MODEL TO
CHASE – INCLUDING GRACE.
(839)

I'M IN A BIND. I
CAN'T FIND WHAT'S LEFT OF MY MIND.
BE KIND -- REWIND ME.
(837)

I'M NOT FINE WITH AGE –
SUPPOSED DECLINE. THAT'S A LINE
I'LL DRAW AND DEFINE.
(836)

DAYDREAMING – WISHING,
WATCHING, SCHEMING – WHILE TIME WELL
SPENT, DOESN'T PAY THE RENT.
(830)

LOOKING IN A MIR-
ROR, NOTHING COULD BE CLEARER:
THE END'S MUCH NEARER.
(829)

TIME SHRINKS AS YEARS
EXPAND. I'VE LOST THE LINKS. MY LIFE'S
A CLUMP OF TWISTED STRANDS.
(828)

WE'RE ALL PURSUING
OUR SCHEMES AT THE EXPENSE OF
SOCIETY'S SEAMS.
(827)

THE ONLY WAY TO
YOUR HEART'S THROUGH THE CANYONS AND
DARK CAVES IN YOUR MIND.
(822)

ARE THERE SPACES BE-
TWEEN DIMENSIONS OR DO THEY
OVERLAP? SLEEP WELL.
(821)

WE TAKE FROM THIS EARTH
WITH NO RETURN, THEREBY IT'S
WRATH AND VENGENCE EARN.
(808)

OUR SEARCH FOR LOGIC
IN A RANDOM COSMOS DE-
FLECTS MAN'S EMPTINESS.
(807)

PAST IS NOW PRESENT
FADING SWIFTLY TO FUTURE.
ALL IS ONE IS ALL.
(786)

NEVER EXPECTING
TO REAP WHAT THEY SOW, MOST
SEE THRILLING HIGHS AND LOWS.
(781)

DWELLING IN A PUR-
PLE HAZE, OUT OF SYNCH, OUT OF
PHASE, WON'T CHANGE MY WAYS.
(776)

WHAT I SHOULD DO OF-
TEN CONFLICTS WITH WHAT I WANT
TO DO. WHAT TO DO?
(775)

REASON OFTEN COMES
AT THE EXPENSE OF HAPPI-
NESS. AND VICE-VERSA.
(774)

NO ONE'S BORN KIND: THAT
EVOLVES THROUGH GOOD EXAMPLES
INSPIRING RESPONSE.
(773)

I'M WAR-GOODS, REFUSE
FROM MAN'S GO TO MEANS OF CON-
FLICT RESOLUTION.
(772)

THE GAME OF LIFE HAS
AN ASSURED END, YET WE ALL
PRETEND – THEM NOT ME.
(771)

THE GAME OF LIFE HAS
NO RULES. IT'S A HUSTLE THAT
DEVOURS CLUELESS FOOLS.
(770)

CERTAINTY HAS TWO
CERTAIN OUTCOMES: DISAPPOINT-
MENT OR MISERY.
(769)

FRIEND? OR FOE? TRUST? OR
BE WARY? THAT'S WHAT WE ALL
NEED TO KNOW. SCARY.
(765)

AFTER ALL THESE YEARS,
MUSIC FROM THE SPHERES SOFTLY
SOOTHES, EASES MY FEARS.
(762)

AGED, ABOUT TO LEAVE
THIS LIFE. SHOULD ONE SMILE OR GRIEVE?
EACH HAS ITS MERITS.
(760)

MY TALE OF WOE? I
KNOW, ALL TOO WELL, I'M
ABOUT TO GO STRAIGHT TO HELL.
(752)

C'MON, WE ALL STRETCH THE
TRUTH. OUR BEST FIBS ARE, AT
LEAST, HALF TRUE. NO LIE!
(751)

IF EVERY BAD
HAS A SILVER LINING, I'M
RICHER THAN MIDAS.
(748)

IF WE'D STOP RE-IN-
VENTING THE WHEEL, MANKIND MIGHT
HAVE A CHANCE TO HEAL.
(746)

CHILDREN'S INNOCENCE
HAUNTS ME. WE HAVE IT, BRIEFLY,
THEN LOSE IT QUICKLY.
(745)

LIFE'S NOT ART – COMPOSED,
ORDERED, CLEAN. IT'S CHAOTIC,
TANGLED, SOMETIMES MEAN.
(744)

LOOK IN A MIRROR.
WHO DO YOU SEE? YOUR BEST FRIEND?
OR AN ENEMY?
(737)

LOSING SELF-RESPECT
WE FREE FALL, OUT OF CONTROL,
TOWARDS THE ABYSS.
(733)

A COMPULSIVE NEED
TO BE 'RIGHT' DEPRIVES OTHERS
OF YOUR KEEN INSIGHT.
(728)

I HOPE – PRAY – THOSE FEW
GOOD DEEDS I'VE DONE SUFFICE, WHEN
MY SCALES ARE BALANCED.
(726)

WE'VE LOST OUR WAY. FAIR
TO SAY RULES OF PLAY ARE REL-
ICS OF YESTERDAY.
(706)

TAKE A LOOK AT HIS-
TORY. LIKE WHAT YOU SEE? WHAT
WAS IS AND WILL BE.
(696)

WE DON'T HAVE TO A-
GREE TO GET ALONG … JUST LET
EACH OTHER BE RIGHT – OR WRONG.
(694)

DEMONS DISRUPT MY
SLEEP – WORSE, NOT CONTENT TO HO-
VER, THEY BURROW DEEP.
(692)

DEFYING LOGIC,
WE BEGUILE OURSELVES ON PATHS
MOST UNTENABLE.
(691)

GREED'S GRIP GOES DEEP IN-
TO A SOUL, FREEZING ITS VIC-
TIMS HEART BLACK AS COAL.
(690)

WELL PAST THE AGE OF
CONSENT, MY TIMES BEST SPENT PON-
DERING HOW THINGS WENT.
(686)

GRAY WITH AGE, BACK BENT,
DAY'S OF RAGE MISSPENT, TIME PLAYS
DESPITE MY DISSENT.
(684)

YOU HAVE A CONSCIENCE.
YOU DON'T CHEAT OR LIE. HOW CAN
YOU BE SUCCESSFUL?
(682)

FOR THOSE WHO HAVE, OR
SEEK, POWER NO SIN'S TOO GREAT
EXCEPT LOSING IT.
(676)

INCESSANT CONTEN-
TIOUSNESS AND WIN AT ALL COSTS
MINDSETS PRESAGE DOOM.
(675)

LOOK AT WHAT'S GOING
ON TODAY. STUDY THE PAST.
WHATS NEW? – BETTER TOYS.
(673)

WHAT WE THINK AND FEEL
ISN'T WHAT WE KNOW. CONFUSING
THESE BRINGS PAIN AND WOE.
(669)

TELL ME, WITHOUT PO-
ETRY IN YOUR SOUL, CAN A
LIFE EVER BE WHOLE?
(666)

PURPLE TWILIGHT SHADES
THE SUN. STARS TWINKLE ON, ONE
BY ONE. NIGHT'S BEGUN.
(655)

SOME CRAVE LIVING ON
EDGE, DEFYING ALL ODDS, DANG-
LING OVER THE LEDGE.
(640)

WHEN THAT BELL TOLLS FOR
ME, I DON'T HAVE TO WORRY.
I'M QUITE DEAF, YOU SEE.
(639)

ATONEMENT AWAITS.
LONG NEGLECTED, ABUSED, OUR EARTH
WILL HAVE ITS REVENGE.
(636)

IF WE EVER GET
A SECOND CHANCE, DO YOU THINK
WE'LL KNOW TO BE KIND?
(633)

GENTLE BREEZE MURMERS
THROUGH THE TREES WHISPERING *"BE
AT REST, TAKE YOUR EASE."*
(586)

INSTINCTIVELY
INCONCEIVABLE, I IM-
AGINE INNOCENCE.
(561)

LAWS, RIGHTS – ALL HUMAN
CONCEITS – DON'T EXIST IN NA-
TURE. JUST LIFE. AND DEATH.
(553)

THE QUESTION ISN'T WILL
MANKIND SURVIVE; IT'S HOW MUCH
LONGER WILL WE LAST.
(550)

WE PREACH LIFE'S PRECIOUS,
WHILE DESTROYING THE EARTH. THINK
SOMETHING'S NOT QUITE RIGHT?
(535)

SELF-PITY CLEANSES
OUR SOUL BY PROVIDING AB-
SOLUTION FROM BLAME.
(524)

TERRIBLE BEAUTIES:
PEACE BY WARFARE; LOVE FROM LOSS;
HOPE THROUGH SUFFERING.
(523)

THESE ARE CERTAIN: DEATH;
NOT KNOWING HOW YOUR *"FRIENDS"* WILL
ACT -- UNTIL THEY DO.
(522)

WEEP FOR US! IT SEEMS
EARTH'S BEYOND REDEMPTION. WE
DID THIS TO OURSELVES.
(514)

WELL, WHAT WE THINK WE
KNOW MIGHT BE SO, BUT WE DON'T
KNOW WHAT WE DON'T KNOW.
(482)

RANDOM THOUGHT: MAYBE
ALL WE SEE AND DO IS SOME
BEING'S PLAY-STATION.
(481)

HOW MANY LIVES HAVE
YOU LIVED? WE ALL LEAD MANY.
IT'S A CONUNDRUM.
(465)

RAIN'S DONE. FRESH, CLEAN AIR.
SUN'S PEEPING, RAINBOW'S JEWELED
HUES MAKE MY HEART DANCE.
(463)

HOW CAN WE LEARN FROM
OUR MISTAKES IF WE DON'T AD-
MIT WE MAKE ANY?
(451)

IF AGE IS JUST A
STATE OF MIND, WHY CAN'T I RE-
MEMBER MY ADDRESS?
(432)

I STRUGGLE TO FIND
RELEVANCE IN A CULTURE
BASED ON ONES -- ZEROS.
(424)

I'M COMPELLED TO SAY
THIS: EACH DAY IT'S MORE CERTAIN
NONE OF US ARE SANE.
(419)

WELL ... MOVIE ICONS
AND ROCK STARS SAY IT'S OK.
HOW CAN WE GO WRONG?
(418)

EVIL'S CONTENT TO
WAIT, SMIRKING, KNOWING THAT FEW
RESIST TEMPTATION.
(417)

COULD STRING THEORY'S
DIMENSIONS BE RELEVANT
TO DANTE'S CIRCLES?
(411)

SLIPPING IN AND OUT
OF DREAMLIKE TRANCES, I CAN'T
BE SURE YOU EXIST.
(410)

LEVITATING, I
HOVER, HESITANT TO LET
GO LIFE'S SPECIOUS HOLD.
(409)

PINING FOR THE *"GOOD
OLE DAYS"* MITIGATES THE GUILT
ENDEMIC TO SLOTH.
(408)

WHAT WE THINK WE KNOW
ABOUT HISTORY WAS WRIT-
TEN BY THE WINNERS.
(404)

NO ONE WHO LACKS CON-
FIDENCE CAN BE SUBTLE OR
GRASP NUANCE CLEARLY.
(396)

DREAMS OR MEMORIES?
FANTASY? REALITY?
WE FLOAT IN AND OUT.
(393)

DELIVER US FROM
PRIDE SWELLING RIGHTEOUSNESS ERE
WE UNLEASH ALL HELL.
(387)

THE MORE GAMES ONE PLAYS
THE SOONER THEIR HOUSE OF CARDS
COLLAPSES. DEAL'EM.
(386)

A WAR ENDS. WE CHEER
YET DON'T REFLECT ON CAUSES.
A NEW WAR STARTS ... DUH!
(385)

ADD UP ALL THE *WHAT
IF'S, MAYBE'S, SHOULDA'S."* THEIR SUM?
OUR UNFULFILLED DREAMS.
(384)

ALL BOOKSMART PEOPLE
KNOW A LOT, BUT THEY'RE NOT AL-
WAYS SMART WHERE IT COUNTS.
(372)

DISCIPLINED, PRINCI-
PLED, I REEL, OUTCAST IN A
WIN-AT-ALL-COSTS WORLD.
(370)

FRET NOT LIFE'S PASSAGE.
'TIS TOO GREAT A BOON TO BE
GRANTED US ONE OFF.
(366)

TODAY'S CONTEXT ISN'T
YESTERDAY'S OR TOMORROW'S.
MEANING'S TIME CONSCIOUS.
(363)

WE WHO EXPECT YOUR
ALL EXPAND THE VOID BETWEEN
OURSELVES AND OTHERS.
(346)

SOON, WE'LL FIND CURES FOR
ALL CONTAGEOUS DISEASES
SAVE THE WORST – POWER.
(332)

HOW WILL IT PLAY FOR
ME? WHERE WILL I BE? WHAT'S THE
LAST THING I'LL HEAR? SEE?
(328)

OTHERS CAN'T SEE US
AS WE SEE OURSELVES. HOW COULD
THEY? THEY'RE OUTSIDE US.
(317)

THE ABYSS BECKONS –
CAN'T RESIST ITS SIREN SONG.
TEETERING – I WAKE.
(315)

IS ALL LIFE PRECIOUS?
A SELECT FEW? JUST YOURS? QUITE
A CAN OF WORMS, HUH?
(312)

PERFECTIONISTS DON'T
ACCEPT HUMAN FRAILTY. WHY
SHOULD THEY? THEY'RE PERFECT!
(308)

MAN'S END GAME? ALIGN
OUR CREATIVE MINDS WITH EARTH'S
LIFE FORCE: HARMONY.
(306)

OLD SOULS' CONDUIT
WISDOM THROUGH TIME'S TRAVERSES.
HEED AND CHERISH THEM.
(295)

IMMAGINATION:
MAN'S HOPE FOR SURVIVAL. NO
VISION, NO FUTURE.
(293)

RAINBOW MIST SWIRLS,
GENTLY COAXING DAWN AWAKE.
ACT I, SCENE I – *DAY*.
(272)

WHAT DO WE HAVE TO
DO TO BRING PEACE TO THIS WORLD?
BEST BET? START OVER.
(217)

HEALTH, LOVE, PEACE OF MIND
SHOULD SUFFICE, BRING CONTENTMENT.
LOOK AROUND. DO THEY?
(212)

QUANDRY: IS A CYN-
ICAL VIEW OF MAN'S NATURE
RIGHT ON OR TOO KIND?
(206)

TRUE LOVE'S A ONE-IN-
A MILLION CRAPSHOOT. BEST TO
STICK WITH THE PONIES.
(204)

YOU SAY MAN'S FUTURE
HAS NO BOUNDS, IS ASSURED? WEEP,
FRAGILE, ONE-OFF EARTH!
(197)

SILVER MOON, CALM SEA,
GENTLE BREEZE CARESSING ME.
STAY! SERENITY.
(194)

HOW TO DEFINE "FAITH":
"BELIEVING WITHOUT SEEING"
OR SPINNING THE WHEEL?
(129)

STARRY, STARRY NIGHT,
IN ITS WONDER AND DELIGHT,
ILLUMINS OUR FRIGHT.
(123)

MOST FLEE FROM SILENCE.
WHY DOES IT FRIGHTEN THEM SO?
DR. FREUD, PLEASE JOIN IN.
(122)

WHAT IF – THESE TWO WORDS
INSPIRE GREATNESS OR CONSPIRE
WITH DOUBT TO CRIPPLE?
(106)

ALONE, PASSING TIME.
BAD CHOICES LEFT FEW OPTIONS.
PRAYING I'LL WISE UP.
(97)

DON'T EXPECT LOGIC.
UNFAMILIAR TO MOST, IT'S
CONSIDERED BY FEW.
(94)

LAWYERS ARE WORDSMITHS.
PRECISE MEANINGS, NOTHING MORE.
I'S DOTTED. *T'S* CROSSED.
(91)

OUR LEGAL SYSTEM
DOESN'T RENDER JUSTICE SILLY;
IT RESOLVES DISPUTES.
(89)

MY DAD NEVER ONCE
HUGGED ME OR SAID HE LOVED ME.
HOW F---ED UP IS THAT?
(71)

*"THE NIGHT IS DARKEST
JUST BEFORE THE DAWN."* FOR MAN,
WHAT TIME IS SUNRISE?
(68)

IF ALL THE WORLD'S A
STAGE AND WE'RE THE ACTORS ... HMMM –
WHO'S THE AUDIENCE?
(63)

UNIVERSAL TRUTHS
OVER-RIDE PERSONAL TRUTH.
SEEMS WE NEVER LEARN?
(58)

LIFE KEEP COMING UP
SEVENS OR SNAKE EYES? ONLY
YOU CONTROL THAT ROLL.
(57)

AT THE VERY END
WHAT WILL BE YOUR FINAL THOUGHT,
LIFE WELL-LIVED -- OR NOT?
(56)

MEMORIES, LIKE TRUTH,
ARE SUBJECTIVE: LESS FACT, MORE
DESIRES LONG SUPPRESSED.
(55)

I WILL NEVER BE
A CAUTIONARY TALE! BRING
IT ON! I'M READY.
(54)

SURVIVING YOUR TEENS
IN SOUND MIND AND TRAUMA FREE
IS EXTREMELY RARE.
(53)

YESTERDAY LINGERS.
TOMORROW'S SURPRISES LOOM.
PAST PREDICTS FUTURE.
(51)

'ROUND AND 'ROUND SHE GOES,
WE CAN'T KNOW WHEN IT'LL STOP: LIFE'S
ROULETTE WHEEL – HOLD ON TIGHT!
(44)

WHAT'S MORE IMPORTANT:
MONEY – POWER, OR: FAMILY -- LOVE?
IT'S NOT EVEN CLOSE!
(41)

DRAGONFLIES JETE;
AEROBATIC AERIALS;
AN ANCIENT BALLET.
(28)

STILL, GLASSY SURFACE.
MIRRORING CREAMY PUFFS,
FLOATING LAZILY.
(27)

MIND IMPRINTS ITS NEEDS:
REASON; CALM; ORDER. HEART HEATS
HEAD. PASSION TRIUMPHS.
(12)

STILL, CLEAR, STARRY NIGHT;
PALE SILVER SLIVER STANDS WATCH;
LOVERS, ENTWINED, KISS
(11)

WISPY CLOUDS DRIFT HIGH;
BIRDS TRILL, WOLVES DANCE 'NEATH BLUE SKIES;
SUSSERANT WIND SIGHS.
(10)

TRUTH'S NOT INTERNAL;
IT'S EXTERNAL TO MIND'S SAY;
AND TOLLS ETERNAL.
(8)

HEALTH FOLLOWS SICKNESS;
AS DOES SPRING THE WINTER SNOW;
WHAT, THEN, AFTER LIFE?
(7)

WE COME IN NAKED,
GRABBING ALL EGO'S PLAYTHINGS,
WE GO OUT NAKED.
(4)

LITTLE ONE'S PLAY WHILE
WITHERED, TEARY EYES MOURN CRUEL
TIME'S TOO SWIFT PASSAGE.
(2)

AUTUMN LEAVES SWIRLING;
OMINOUS GRAY CLOUDS HOVER
CHILLING SUMMER'S HOPES.
(1)

BOOK THREE

LOVE AND LOSS

ACT I

On the Road to Romance

YOUR LIGHTNESS OF BE-
ING HAS ME SEEING THAT I,
TOO, COULD SOAR WITH YOU.
(1991)

MET A GIRL, HAD A
WHIRL. FUN! SOON DONE. MORAL? LIFE'S
THAT WAY: DAY-TO-DAY.
(1990)

RUDDERLESS, FATE'S WINDS
NUDGE ME ALONG, ENTRANCED BY
MY LATEST SYREN'S SONG.
(1964)

I SEE YOU. MY HEART
PUMPS FASTER: JUST ONE THUMP CLO-
SER TO DISASTER.
(1963)

LOOPED MY LASSO ON-
TO YOU(R) WHIRLWIND. DON'T KNOW HOW
IT'LL END. PULL ME IN!
(1950)

PROSPECTING FOR HEARTS,
I MINE LOVE'S LOST ARTS: CARING,
SHARING – LIFE'S BEST PARTS.
(1867)

"I DO" IS TRUE – IN
THE MOMENT. TIME RE-SCRIPTS OUR
"TRUE", EVEN *"I DO."*
(1746)

AN OPEN WINDOW,
EXCITING, MAY BE INVI-
TING YOU TO SORROW.
(1722)

YOU'RE NOT WHO I THOUGHT.
I BOUGHT INTO YOUR VIVA-
CITY. SILLY ME.
(1701)

YOU HAVE ENVIA-
BLE ADDICTIONS: NO SHAME AND
NO INHIBITIONS.
(1607)

IF IT ITCHES, SCRATCH.
IF IT HURTS, CRY. IF IT'S LOVE
HUG, KISS, SCREAM *"GOODBYE!"*
(1575)

YOU AND ME. COFFEE.
WE'LL DISCUSS WHAT MIGHT POSSI-
BLY BE. YOU AND ME?
(1567)

ECSTACY, RARELY
FELT, PERFECTLY DESCRIBES ME
SEEING WE ... I MELT.
(1549)

CHEMISTRY 'TWIXT TWO
SOULS IS, AT BEST, SOPHISTRY;
AT WORST, TWO FOOLS CURSED.
(1522)

YOU'RE NOT TO BLAME. BLINDED
BY YOUR FLAME, I PURSUED. CHA-
OS ENSUED ... PRELUDE.
(1520)

IN CASE I FORGET,
PLEASE KNOW I LOVE YOU. (IT MIGHT
HAPPEN, BUT ... NOT YET.)
(1486)

BEAUTY ABIDE IN
ME. FLEE NOT BEFORE EGO'S
CONCEIT AND FRAILTY.
(1348)

ON LOVE THERE'S NO EX-
PERT. BY ITS VERY NATURE
IT DEFIES CONCERT.
(1289)

LOVE'S FOREPLAY. MORE DIF-
FICULT: STAYING TOGETHER
AS YEARS FADE AWAY.
(1282)

LOVE: THE PRICE ONE PAYS
TO PLAY IS, OFTEN, MORE THAN
IF THEY STAYED AWAY.
(1278)

IN MY DEEPEST RE-
CESSES, ONE THOUGHT POSSESSES
ME: YOUR CARESSES.
(1269)

AT THE END OF MY
RUN, WHEN IT'S ALL SAID AND DONE,
YOU'LL STILL BE THE ONE.
(1101)

YOU MAKE MY HEART DANCE,
MY SOUL SING. YOU ENHANCE EV-
ERYTHING I AM.
(1068)

BEFORE YOU, I HAD
A PLAN. SINCE YOU IT'S IN THE
CAN. NEW PLAN – WE TWO.
(1057)

YOU PLAY ME IN PER-
FECT HARMONY. YOU KNOW MY
CHORDS, MY KEY. BRAVA!
(1051)

MINE'S THE QUEST FOR A
PERFECT LOVE THAT CAN'T EXIST.
STILL … I WILL PERSIST.
(1045)

MY LIFE'S CORK POPPING
AND BED HOPPING. FUN – WHILE IT
LASTS. I'M AGING FAST.
(1039)

STOKE MY FIRE. FILL ME
WITH DESIRE. TAKE ME HIGHER –
OR TAKE A FLYER!
(1028)

THE BEST IT EVER
WILL BE IS EACH DAY YOU'RE IN
LOVE, HEALTHY AND FREE.
(1019)

EYES CLOSED – YOU. OPEN --
YOU. BRIGHT DAY – YOU. DARK NIGHT – YOU.
I LIVE, I BREATHE – YOU.
(1008)

LOVE, FLEETING, FRAGILE,
RARELY WORTH ITS COST, CAN BRING
MUCH PAIN, GREATER LOSS.
(994)

ROMANCE: A DANCE BE-
TWEEN TWO STRUTTERS PUTTING ON
A SHOW. ALL EGO.
(965)

A LADY WHO HAS
GOOD FORM KNOWS FEW WILL OPPOSE
HER IF SHE SHOWS IT.
(918)

NOUGHT MAKETH MINE HEART
SING MORE THAN THAT JOY AND WARMTH`
THY SWEET LOVE DOTH BRING.
(870)

IT'S TOO SOON. WE'RE NOT
IN TUNE. BEST WAIT, FIND THE LINKS,
SLOWLY GET IN SYNCH.
(817)

I DON'T YEARN FOR YOU.
I BURN! SEEING YOU LIGHTS ME
ON FIRE WITH DESIRE.
(809)

YOU'RE INSPIRING 'THO
YOUR CONSTANT INQUIRING CAN
BE, AT TIMES, TIRING.
(789)

FOLLOW YOUR HEART – FOR
THE MOST PART. BE SMART. DON'T LET
IT TEAR YOU APART.
(779)

ONE OF THESE DAYS WE'LL
MEET AGAIN. NOT SURE WHERE OR WHEN.
I'LL DREAM 'TIL THEN.
(778)

BE BOLD IN LOVE. STAY
ON THE ATTACK. GROW OLD WITH
LOVE. HOLD NOTHING BACK.
(777)

THINK YOU KNOW ALL THERE
IS TO KNOW ABOUT SOMEONE?
WAKE UP? YOU'RE DREAMING.
(768)

YOUNG, SWEET, TENDER LOVE
CAN BECOME BRITTLE ABSENT
CONSTANT NURTURING.
(613)

TO GET TO HAPPI-
LY EVER AFTER – EMBRACE
THIS TIGHT: 'LET'S WORK HARD.'
(612)

I KNEW YOU BEFORE
WE MET. YOU'RE THE ONE MY DREAMS
WOULDN'T LET ME FORGET.
(599)

IN THE TEMPLE OF
MY SOUL DWELLS MY SAVING GRACE:
A PURE LOVE FOR YOU.
(566)

YOU KNOW I LOVE YOU.
YOU SHOULD UNDERSTAND WHY I
CAN'T COMMIT JUST YET.
(503)

YOU BEGUILE, INTRIGUE
AND CONFUSE ME. CAN'T TALK OR
THINK. GOTTA BE LOVE.
(500)

COLD, CLEAR TWINKLING NIGHT:
SNOW GLISTENS, MOONLIGHT BRIGHT. A
HEART'S-IN-LOVE DELIGHT.
(486)

ALONG WITH GOOD HEALTH,
CHOOSE LOVE OVER EVERY-
THING ELSE IN THIS LIFE.
(483)

LOVE'S SCARY. IT'S NOT
EASY; SO MESSY. BUT, OH,
WOW! IT'S WONDERFUL.
(478)

EVIDENCE ABOUNDS
THAT FEW OF US STAY MARRIED.
WHY GO DOWN THAT PATH?
(477)

I HAD A PLAN AND
WAS ALL SET TO ROLL THEN WHAM!
I DIDN'T PLAN ON YOU!
(458)

I PROMISE TO LOVE,
HONOR, AND OBEY YOU – BUT,
JUST 'TIL WE DIVORCE.
(437)

LOVE'S FRAGILE. THAT THIN
LINE BETWEEN IN AND OUT'S LIKE
TIGHTROPE BALANCING.
(421)

MY HEART, MY SOUL ARE
YOUR'S TO PLAY WITH AS YOU WILL.
PLEASE HANDLE WITH CARE.
(414)

TELL ME HOW YOU FEEL.
I MIGHT NOT WANT TO HEAR IT,
BUT I NEED TO KNOW.
(401)

CARESS ME WITH PAS-
SION. POSSESS ME WITH INTEL-
LECT. CAPTURE MY SOIL.
(399)

PULL ME CLOSE! HOLD ME
TIGHT! PROTECT ME FROM MY SELF-
IMPOSED LIFE LONG FRIGHT.
(397)

TRUE LOVE'S SOME GET, A
WHOLE LOTTA GIVE. IT AIN'T REAL
ANY OTHER WAY.
(373)

YOU'RE THE ONE FOR ME.
IT'S NOT MUTUAL, BUT WE
HAD OUR TIME. THANK YOU.
(364)

AN ABIDING LOVE'S
DEFINED BY PASSION, SUSTAINED
BY SHARED COMPASSION.
(359)

MY HEART STARTS POUNDING,
MY EYES WELL UP, MY SOUL SINGS
WHEN YOU SMILE AT ME.
(348)

MOST PEOPLE AREN'T RO-
MANTICS – IT'S WAY TO NUANCED.
YOU FEW – DON'T GIVE IN.
(344)

THERE'S TWO WAYS TO VIEW
LOVE: IT'S EVERYTHING OR
AN ABERRATION.
(324)

IN MY MIND'S EYE I'M
YOUR KIND OF GUY. IN YOUR'S I'M
A HASTY *"GOODBYE!"*
(285)

MY MIND GOES BLANK, MY
HEART'S ABLAZE, ENTHRALLED, INFLAMED,
BY YOUR PIERCING GAZE.
(266)

LOVE'S NOT LOGICAL.
CHEMISTRY'S PRIMEVAL, BE-
YOND PLANS AND INTENT.
(264)

MOST OF US SHARE LOVE'S
ILLUSIONS AND DELUSIONS.
TOO FEW KNOW TRUE LOVE.
(255)

BE NOT CONTENT
WITH BAUBLES AND FINERY.
REACH HIGHER. SEIZE LOVE!
(234)

THE HEART KNOWS WHAT MOST
MINDS DARE NOT SAY: WITHOUT LOVE
WE'RE HARD, CRUMBLING CLAY.
(228)

LET ME BUT REFLECT
ON YOUR GENTLE, CARING SELF
AND CONTENTMENT'S MINE.
(227)

TRUE LOVE CAN'T BE BOUGHT.
IT'S EITHER GIVEN OR EARNED.
THIS WILL NEVER CHANGE.
(165)

LISTEN TO YOUR HEART.
IT KNOWS WHAT YOUR MIND WON'T SAY:
LOVE DEFIES LOGIC.
(126)

EYES ONLY FOR YOU.
TWO HEARTS, ONE LOVE – FOREVER!
NONSENSE! IT WON'T LAST.
(110)

LOGIC OR PASSION?
BOTH? EITHER? YOUR CHOICE TO MAKE.
THERE'S NO WRONG ANSWER.
(109)

REMEMBERING YOU,
I SHAKE UNCONTROLLABLY.
HOT TEARS DROWN MY HEART.
(93)

WITHOUT YOU, SHADOWS
COMPRESS MY EVERY SECOND.
YOU ARE MY LIFE-LIGHT.
(86)

GO AHEAD! PLAY YOUR GAMES.
I'M NOT EASILY BROKEN.
JUST DON'T LET ME GO.
(85)

PICTURES IN MY MIND
KEEP CONNECTING ME TO YOU,
LEAVING ME NO PEACE!
(83)

PLEASE! DON'T SAY *"I DO"*
UNLESS YOUR HEART SAYS HE/SHE
IS A LIFETIME'S NEED.
(64)

THANKS FOR BEING MY
FRIEND. YOU HAVE MADE MY WORLD RIGHT.
THERE AREN'T WORDS ENOUGH.
(60)

DISTANCE MAKES THE HEART
GROW FONDER – FOR A WHILE. THEN
IT TENDS TO WANDER!
(47)

HOLDING ONTO PAIN
DEADENS YOUR SOUL, LEAVES YOU EMPTY.
GOT TO LET IT GO.
(46)

LAUGHING, HEARTS OPEN;
CHILDREN LIFE'S MEANING CONVEY;
GIVING, SHARING LOVE.
(9)

NEW LOVE'S ENTICEMENTS
CAPTIVATE MIND'S REASONING,
FOR BETTER OR WORSE.
(3)

ACT II

In the Eye of the Storm

TWO SHIPS IN THE NIGHT,
WE COLLIDED. TWISTED, BURNT, SPENT, WE
SILENTLY SUBSIDED.
(2087)

I CAN'T CONCEIVE WHY
I DIDN'T BELIEVE YOU. HOW COULD
I BE SO NAÏVE?
(2045)

I FEEL YOUR SCREAM, HEAR
YOUR TOUCH, WANT TO SEE YOU NOT
VERY MUCH. LET'S TEXT.
(2022)

I SEE CLEARLY: YOU'RE
TOO MUCH FOR ME. THERE'S NOTHING
WRONG WITH YOU – JUST "WE."
(1952)

I THOUGHT I KNEW YOU.
MY BAD. THEN I LEARNED THE TRUE
YOU. NOW, IT'S MY SAD.
(1909)

BUSY BEING *'FREE'*,
AND ANGRY, WE IGNORE WHAT'S
IN STORE FOR OUR KIDS.
(1900)

WHEN WILL IT BE ME?
IT'S ALWAYS BEEN YOU. WHEN WILL
YOU SEE I'M HERE TOO?
(1895)

LOOK AROUND. WHAT DO
YOU SEE? I CAN GUARANTEE
ONE THING – IT ISN'T WE.
(1876)

SO, YOU KNOW MY TALE
OF WOE DIDN'T BEGIN WITH YOU.
IT MIGHT END THERE THOUGH.
(1840)

TO GET UNSTUCK, I'VE
GOT TO RUN AWAY FROM US.
IF I DON'T, I'M DONE.
(1815)

YOU DON'T COMMUNI-
CATE, YOU DICTATE, WITH INTENT
TO DOMINATE. BYE!
(1800)

IT'S CURIOUS AND
MYSTERIOUS THAT YOU WON'T
SEE THE OBVIOUS.
(1799)

WHY WON'T YOU LET US
BE US. WE LET YOU BE YOU
WITH NO FUSS. C'MON!
(1796)

IN ALL SINCEREI-
TY, YOU'RE A RARITY: MOST DON'T
LIE BLATENTLY.
(1737)

I SHOULD'VE KNOWN WE'D BE
BLOWN WHEN YOU ANSWERED YOUR PHONE,
WHILE WE WERE KISSING.
(1733)

PONDERING US, I
PERJURE MY PRIDE TO AVOID
BEING SWEPT ASIDE.
(1726)

LOVE CEASES WHEN LIFE
ERODES ITS VITAL PIECES,
WE, INTO YOU/ME.
(1721)

CREATIVE THINKING:
LYING AS JUSTIFYING;
PREACHING AS TEACHING.
(1700)

THE TRAGEDY OF
WE IS THAT I CANNOT BE
SOMEONE I'M NOT – YOU.
(1699)

OUR DEMISE NIGH, WHO
KNOWS WHAT WILL ARISE FROM THE
CHAOS WE'VE DEVISED?
(1689)

THE RIGHT SAYS *"ME"*. THE
LEFT SAYS *"WE."* THERE'S NO MIDDLE
GROUND. WE'RE ALL HELL-BOUND.
(1687)

DISSENT WITHIN A
COMMON CAUSE, BEGS INTENT AND
AGENDAS HIDDEN.
(1679)

YOUR EAST IS MY WEST.
YOUR LEAST IS MY BEST. I FAIL
YOUR EASIEST TEST.
(1677)

TRAUMA I'M USED TO.
DRAMA? NOTHIN' NEW. AND, WOW!
I'VE GOT BOTH IN YOU.
(1670)

SOME PARTS OF ME SEE
THAT WE CAN NO LONGER BE;
THE REST DISAGREE.
(1628)

YOU LET ME BE ME.
I LET YOU BE YOU. SIMPLE,
YES? ALAS … NOT TRUE.
(1585)

I DON'T THINK THE WAY
YOU SAY, I SHOULD. WHO'S THE ONE
WHO'S MISUNDERSTOOD?
(1584)

YOU USE WORDS. I CHOOSE
HUES. LOGIC FADES AS SHADES OF
GRAY DIFFUSE OUR VIEWS.
(1580)

THOSE SPELLS YOU CAST AREN'T
MEANT TO LAST. YOU TAKE WHAT YOU
NEED, THEN – GONE! LIGHT SPEED.
(1503)

THE THINGS WE SHARE ARE
CAST ASIDE AS SELF-INTER-
EST INFLATES OUR PRIDE.
(1480)

WHY SHOULD I BE LIKE
YOU? WHY WOULD I WANT TO? BOTH
DIFFERENT: STILL *"WE."*
(1438)

THE TIME TO CRY IS
AFTER YOU SAY, *"GOOD BYE."* 'TIL
THEN, GRIN – MIGHT STILL WIN.
(1436)

YOU'RE TORTUOUS RAP-
TURE! IT PAINS ME YOU
CAPTURED ME SO EASILY.
(1419)

FOR YOUR MIND BENT THERE'S
JUST ONE ASSIGNMENT: SOLI-
TARY CONFINEMENT.
(1413)

MY TAKE? THE TIME IT
TAKES TO MAKE UP IS BETTER
SPENT MAKING IT WORK.
(1412)

FUTURE'S IN DOUBT; PRES-
ENT'S A ROUT; NOT SURE WHAT LIFE'S
ALL ABOUT … I POUT.
(1409)

I CRY A LOT MORE
THAN I OUGHT. MOST: SORROWS. SOME:
FEWER TOMORROWS.
(1408)

I SEE WHAT'S GOING
ON. IT'S UGLY. DECISION
TIME: STAY? FLEE? I'M GONE!
(1407)

ME: COMING, GOING,
TO-AND-FROING ... NEVER KNOW-
ING HOW TO SLOW. YOU?
(1402)

YOU'RE A USER – GET
YOUR WAY, DON'T CARE WHAT OTHERS
SAY ... WHO'S THE LOSER?
(1369)

COMEDY IS TO
TRAGEDY, AS YOU ARE TO ME.
YOU LAUGH. I CRY. WHY?
(1326)

DON'T TRY TO SHROUD YOUR
BARREN SOUL FROM ME. WITHOUT
LOOKING, I CAN SEE.
(1321)

PRETEND TO CHEER ME.
SUSPEND REALITY. TRY.
HEAR ME. JUST THIS ONCE.
(1300)

OUR PATHS WON'T MERGE. TAN-
GENT, THEY'LL SOON DIVERGE, BLESSING
US WITH THIS MOMENT.
(1298)

I'VE THOUGHT ABOUT US
A LOT. IT'S WHAT WE'RE NOT THAT
MAKES ME SCREAM, *"I'M CAUGHT."*
(1273)

GO AWAY! I DON'T
WANT TO PLAY. WE ALWAYS HAVE
TO DO WHAT YOU SAY.
(1256)

WHISPER SOFTLY IN
MY EAR WORDS YOU KNOW I NEED
TO HEAR. CALM THE FEAR.
(1251)

WHAT IS, CAN'T BE. WE
KNOW WHAT SHOULD BE, BUT CAN'T/WON'T
WORK IN HARMONY.
(1178)

YOU HAVE TO WIN. I
WANT TO SURVIVE. SO, I GIVE
IN, TO STAY ALIVE.
(1167)

THE PART OF ME THAT
THINKS, SCREAMS *"NO!"* THE HEART OF ME
THAT FEELS, CAN'T LET GO.
(1158)

TRY AS WE MIGHT, WE'LL
NEVER GET IT RIGHT. ALL WE
EVER DO IS FIGHT.
(1150)

AIN'T IT STRANGE HOW EACH
TIME WE PROMISE TO CHANGE, WE
BECOME MORE THE SAME?
(1131)

THY BEAUTY CANNOT
TEMPT ME NOR THY SMILE BEGUILE
ME. GET THEE HENCE. FLEE!
(1124)

IT'S A MYSTERY
TO ME, WHY YOU CAN'T SEE THAT
WE WERE MEANT TO BE.
(1091)

I'M NOT YOU – NEVER
HAVE BEEN. WHY KEEP PLAYING A
GAME, I CANNOT WIN?
(1087)

YOU WOULDN'T LISTEN. WHAT
NOW? WE'VE GOT TO FIND A WAY
OUT OF THIS – SOMEHOW.
(1080)

YOU SIGHED *"I LOVE US."*
WE TRIED. YOU LEFT. I LIED *"WHO
CARES?"* – THEN DIED INSIDE.
(1077)

GLIB, RAZOR TONGUED, THE
EASE WITH WHICH YOU DISPATCH YOUR
ENEMIES ASTOUNDS!
(1052)

YOUR LIGHT'S NOT MINE. YOUR
TRUTH'S DON'T SHINE ONLY. YOU BE
YOU AND I'LL BE ME.
(1040)

DETERMINED TO WIN,
I'LL NEVER GIVE IN, JUST GET
UP AND TRY AGAIN.
(1038)

WHAT'S THE COST OF US?
CONSTANT YELLING AND FUSS, BIG
TEARS, FEW SMILES, NO TRUST.
(1037)

O.K. IN MY DE-
FENSE LET ME SAY: YOU KNEW I
WAS THIS WAY. O.K.?
(1029)

WE CAN'T GET ALONG.
THERE'S NO COMPROMISE. I'M RIGHT.
YOU'RE WRONG. NO ONE TRIES.
(1026)

THE EASE WITH WHICH YOU
DISMISS US SEALS IT. THERE'S NO-
THING LEFT TO DISCUSS.
(1006)

GOTTA DANCE AND SHOUT!
JUST FOUND OUT YOU'RE LEAVING – THAT'S
WHAT IT'S ALL ABOUT.
(1001)

I SWEAR I KNEW IT
WAS YOU! HOW COULD I NOT HAVE
SEEN, NOT HAVE A CLUE?
(999)

I WANT YOU. YOU DON'T
WANT ME TO WANT YOU. WONDER
WHOSE WANT WILL WIN.
(971)

DO YOU SEE HOW I
SEE? I SEE WE. DO YOU SEE
WE OR YOU, THEN ME?
(961)

SURE! I CARE ABOUT
WHAT YOU THINK – IF I AGREE
WITH IT. IF NOT – SHUSSH.
(925)

STARTS RARELY FORETELL
ENDINGS. OH! IF WE COULD BUT
SEE HOW THINGS WILL BE.
(896)

THE PRICE OF GIVING
IN, NOT BEING TRUE TO YOU?
A LIFE OF WHAT -- IFS.
(895)

IT'S IN THE EYES. THEY
DENY THE LIES WITH THEIR
LIPS – NEVER THOSE EYES.
(888)

IF I COULD INSANE
BE, SURELY, I'D SEE WHY YOU
THINK SO LOW OF ME.
(885)

I NEED TO KNOW IF
WE HAVE PLANS TO GROW OR SHOULD
I PACK UP AND GO?
(872)

I ALWAYS WANTED SOME-
ONE JUST LIKE YOU. NOW THAT I
DO, I HAVEN'T A CLUE.
(862)

YOURS ARE THE EYES OF
PERFECT DISGUISE. NO ONE WHO
TRIES SEES THROUGH THE LIES.
(842)

AVOID THIS ALWAYS:
TOO MUCH "ME", RARELY "WE", I,
OR YOU'LL BE LONELY.
(829)

THERE'S NO DOUBT YOU WANT
ME TO GO. I DON'T KNOW WHY
YOU WON'T JUST SAY SO.
(826)

HOW MANY TRIES TO
GET IT RIGHT … FOUR, FORTY-FOUR?
YOU'VE HAD THOSE – AND MORE!
(825)

JUST IN CASE THIS IS
OUR ONLY SHOT, GIVE IT EV-
ERY THING YOU'VE GOT.
(824)

I SEE. YOU BLAME ME.
WHAT ABOUT PERSONAL RE-
SPONSIBILITY.
(819)

I EXIST BETWEEN
REALITY AND FANTA-
SY. CAN YOU SEE ME?
(818)

WHEN WILL I KNOW IT'S
TIME TO GO? HOW DO YOU DO
WHAT YOU DON'T WANT TO DO?
(816)

RUNNING; FEAR FROZEN,
IF LIFE DOESN'T GET ME FIRST, YOU
WILL. WHICH IS THE WORST?
(794)

I COULDN'T. I WOULDN'T. I
SHAN'T. I WILL NOT EVER LET
YOU GO. I JUST CAN'T.
(793)

I KNOW A LOT: I
LOVE YOU, YOU DON'T LOVE ME. WISH
I WASN'T SO KNOWING.
(792)

I'M NOT ENOUGH FOR
YOU. NEVER WILL BE. YOU WANT
PERFECTION, NOT ME.
(782)

NO MORE ALIBIS!
NO MORE LIES! GO! DON'T BOTHER
WITH THE PHONY GOODBYES.
(761)

I WISH I KNEW WHAT
TO DO TO GET THROUGH TO YOU.
HELP ME MAKE US NEW!
(758)

I THOUGHT ABOUT IT.
CAN'T. LIFE WOULDN'T BE WORTH LIVING
IF I GAVE YOU UP.
(747)

NEARING CONCLUSION
I SEE MY DELUSION OF
INCLUSION AS FARCE.
(742)

IF YOU KNOW HOW TO
FIND PEACE OF MIND WITHOUT LOVE
PLEASE! PLEASE! TELL ME NOW.
(741)

I DON'T KNOW WHAT TO
DO WITHOUT YOU. I DON'T KNOW
WHAT TO DO WITH YOU.
(740)

YOU TOOK MY PASSIONS
AND CONVICTIONS AND TURNED THEM
INTO AFFLICTIONS.
(739)

WHERE I SEE US YOU
SEE YOU, THEN ME. NOT MUCH CHANCE
THERE'LL EVER BE *"WE."*
(738)

IF YOU DON'T GIVE WHAT
YOU WANT, WHY WOULD YOU EXPECT
TO GET WHAT YOU WANT?
(734)

YOU'RE SAFE. THERE'S NO WAY
YOU'LL EVER GET OVER YOUR-
SELF. YOU CAN'T GET HURT.
(674)

CAN'T KEEP UP THIS FIGHT-
LOVE-FIGHT GAME. GIMME LOVE-LOVE-
LOVE OR GIMME GONE.
(664)

FUNNY, URBANE, BLESSED
WITH CHARM, YOUR RELENTLESS LIES
RESULT IN DIRE HARM.
(658)

I'VE GOT TO LET US
GO. EACH DAY IS ONE MORE STEP
TOWARDS THE ABYSS.
(657)

IT WAS AN ACCI-
DENT! NOT ON PURPOSE. WHY'RE YOU
COMPLAINING? NO BLOOD.
(654)

DO I DARE? IS IT
POSSIBLE TO BEAR THE PAIN
THAT COMES WITH *"I CARE?"*
(653)

DON'T DISSEMBLE! I CAN
TAKE YOUR BEST AND YOUR WORST.
AT LEAST BE HONEST.
(652)

NOT KNOWING WHAT I
DON'T KNOW, I KNOW THIS: YOU
DON'T SEEM TO KNOW MUCH.
(649)

PART OF ME WANTS TO
SMASH YOU, PART WANTS YOUR HEAD. ALL
OF ME WANTS YOU BACK.
(647)

OUTSIDE, ALL COOL, CALM.
INSIDE I'M TWISTED AND TIED, BLACK
RAGE PERSONIFIED.
(646)

I LOVE US. BUT THAT'S
NOT ENOUGH FOR YOU. WHAT IS?
DO YOU EVEN KNOW?
(645)

I'M GONNA GO NOW.
WE GAVE IT OUR BEST SHOT. AT
LEAST WE TRIED. LOVE YOU.
(644)

YOU ASK TOO MUCH. MY
LOVE, ALL THAT I POSSESS, YES.
YOU CAN'T HAVE MY SOUL.
(643)

THOSE WORDS I LONG TO
HEAR, YOU WON'T SAY, BECAUSE YOU
DON'T LOVE ME THAT WAY.
(642)

IF I SNEEZE OR BLINK
I'LL MISS ALL THERE IS TO HEAR
OR SEE ABOUT YOU.
(620)

WHEN YOU FIGURE OUT
HOW WE'RE GONNA GET ALONG,
SEND ME A POSTCARD.
(618)

I DON'T WANT TO GIVE
IN LESS THAN I DON'T WANT TO
FIGHT. O.K., YOU WIN.
(611)

GO AHEAD. ASK ME.
I'LL GIVE YOU ANSWERS. JUST MAKE
SURE YOU WANT TO KNOW.
(606)

IF THERE'S A KEY TO
UNLOCK YOUR HEART, NO ONE'S BEEN
ABLE TO FIND IT.
(605)

ALL THIS TIME, WE'VE BEEN
FOOLING OURSELVES. I DON'T KNOW
WHO YOU ARE. DO YOU?
(603)

YOU SPIN WEBS, I BE-
LIEVE'EM. I SPIN WEBS, YOU UN-
WEAVE THEM. BELIEVE ME.
(602)

NEXT TO LOVE, BEING
CIVIL AND GETTING ALONG
IS US AT OUR BEST.
(597)

YOU'RE NEVER OFF MY
MIND. I PRETEND WE'RE THROUGH. RIGHT!
THAT JUST WON'T HAPPEN.
(585)

"HAPPINESS IS A
STATE OF MIND." IT'S YOUR MIND. DO
TELL, WHO'S GOT CONTROL?
(582)

HAS IT EVER CROSSED
YOUR MIND THAT YOU'RE NOT ALWAYS
RIGHT? I DON'T THINK SO.
(579)

DON'T TRY TO TELL ME
HOW TO LIVE MY LIFE. YOU'RE NOT
ME. HOW COULD YOU KNOW?
(576)

WOULD YOU PLEASE IGNORE
WHAT YOU SAW. APOLOGIES.
LET ME MAKE IT RIGHT.
(573)

SO, WHEN I TOLD HER
I LOVED HER, SHE RETORTED *"WHAT
THE HELL'S WRONG WITH YOU?"*
(565)

THIS ISN'T WORKING. LOVE'S
NOT ENOUGH. THERE'S GOT TO BE
A WAY. TALK TO ME!
(547)

"IT'S NOT YOU. IT'S ME."
I'VE GOT SOME ISSUES THAT I'M
TRYING HARD TO FIX.
(502)

LET'S REVIEW THE PART
WHERE YOU SAID *"I LOVE AND WANT
YOU, BUT NEED MY SPACE."*
(501)

OUR LIFE'S A PERFOR-
MANCE PIECE. WE'RE EACH OTHER'S AUD-
IENCE AND CRITICS.
(395)

YOU ARE HERE. I AM
HERE. WE ARE HERE. WHEN WILL WE
ACCEPT EACH OTHER?
(394)

AS LONG AS IT'S US
AND THEM THERE CAN BE NO PEACE.
IT'S WE OR CHAOS.
(361)

MY ATTEMPTS TO RE-
CONCILE ARE REBUFFED BY YOUR
BLANK, ICY DISTAIN.
(360)

I'M ON MY KNEES CRAWL-
ING ON THE GROUND. YOU'VE BROKEN
ME, ALL THE WAY DOWN.
(342)

IT TOOK WE TO MAKE
THREE. YES, YOU'RE A MOM, BUT DAD'S
STILL HERE. REMEMBER?
(337)

I'M WITH YOU, BUT WE'RE
NOT TOGETHER SINCE YOU LOST
ALL RESPECT FOR US.
(309)

IN MY GRIEF AND DES-
PAIR YOU'RE NOT THERE. WHY CAN'T I
ACCEPT YOU DON'T CARE?
(300)

RIGHT? WRONG? ONLY IF
YOU'RE CAUGHT. IF NOT, DO AS YOU
WILL. HOW DID WE GET HERE?
(281)

RUSH TO ANGER HAS
REPLACED DON'T BE QUICK TO JUDGE.
WHERE'S OUR COMMON SENSE?
(279)

WE PLAY AT BEING
CIVIL: A CHARADE TO HELP
SOOTHE OUR SAVAGE SOULS.
(278)

THE CHILL OF WINTER'S
NOUGHT COMPARED TO THE ICY STARE
OF YOUR HARD, BLUE EYES.
(233)

IT'S THE MIDDLE OF
THE NIGHT. I'M ALONE, AFRAID.
I DREAM YOU. ALL'S WELL.
(219)

WAIT! YOU SAY I MUST
THINK OF OTHERS BESIDES ME.
HOW ODD. WHY WOULD I?
(216)

SPARE ME YOUR PREACHING!
ALLOW ME FREEDOM OF CHOICE
AS I DO YOU. PLEASE.
(210)

FICKLE, WHIMSICAL,
LOVE BLOWS HOT AND COLD WHILE WE
PRETEND TO KNOW WHY.
(171)

THINK BEING LONELY
IS SAD? IT'S NOTHING COMPARED
WITH BEING UNLOVED.
(168)

WHEN WE TRY TO TALK
NO MATTER WHAT I'M SAYING
YOU JUST WON'T LISTEN.
(100)

LET'S PLAY "THE BLAME GAME!"
TOO FEW OF US KNOW "THE RULE":
IT'S – "THE BUCK STOPS HERE!"
(98)

IF YOU COULD BUT SEE
JUST HOW MUCH I ADORE YOU,
YOU'D GIVE ME A BREAK!
(95)

ACT III

After the Storm

LET'S COMMUNICATE
AND COOPERATE, NOT HATE
AND EXASCERBATE.
(2104)

TO WHOM ARE WE TRUE?
START WITH YOU, EXAMINING
HOW. WHO'S KIDDING WHO?
(2099)

HOW COULD IT BE THAT
YOU WOULD, SILENTLY, ABAN-
DON *"WE"* – SHAMELESSLY?
(2098)

INSTINCTIVELY, I
CRINGE FROM THEE: A GLINT, MERE HINT
OF MALICE THERE BE.
(2082)

I'VE NOT BEEN GRANTED TRUE
LOVE. IS IT THAT I'M UNWOR-
THY OR ... UNLUCKY.
(2078)

I YEARN TO BE HALF
OF A 'WE':SO FAR THAT IS
STILL A DREAM FOR ME.
(2060)

LET'S HUG, REMINISCE,
SHARE WHAT WE'LL MISS ERE LEAPING
FROM LIFE'S PRECIPICE.
(2020)

I THOUGHT WE WERE WHAT
I SOUGHT. SADLY, WE WERE NOT.
WHO WOULDA THOUGHT, HUH?
(1985)

WHAT WE DREAMED WOULD BE
DESTINY WAS A DAY TRIP
IN OUR LIVE'S JOURNEY.
(1955)

I'VE LOST AT LOVE, MOST
OF LIFE, WAR. I'M NOT GONNA
QUIT. THAT'S WHAT HOPE'S FOR.
(1954)

GETTING WHAT I WANT?
EASY. GETTING WHO I WANT?
THEY NEVER WANTED ME.
(1953)

MY ODE TO THE MON-
OLITH THAT'S YOUR BRAIN: *"NOUGHT, BUT
MYTH DOTH IT RETAIN."*
(1948)

WHAT WE CAME FOR WE
COULDN'T GET. WHO'S TO BLAME FOR IT?
NO ONE WAS A FIT.
(1942)

BEING WELL-SCHOOLED, I'M
RARELY FOOLED. BRAVO! YOU COOLED
MY INFLAMED EGO.
(1938)

WHAT IT WAS AIN'T NO
MORE. WHAT IT FEELS LIKE IS A
CHORE. DON'T SLAM THE DOOR.
(1872)

THOUGHT YOU WERE GONE. WRONG.
BACK – AGAIN. THOUGHT MY PAIN WAS
GONE. WRONG. BACK – AGAIN.
(1854)

THE ONE I KNEW ISN'T
YOU. WHERE DID SHE GO? WHY? WOULD
THAT IT WERE NOT SO.
(1833)

THE BEST OF ME WAS
GIVEN TO YOU. THE REST OF
ME, I'LL GIVE TO ME.
(1821)

AS THE YEARS SPEED BY
LARGER TEARS FLOW FROM MY EYES ...
SORROWS REALIZED.
(1806)

TIME TO PAY MY RAN-
SOM; THAT PIPER'S BILL'S DUE. I
LOST. THOSE PAINS CAME TRUE.
(1720)

I DON'T MISS MUCH. JUST
THESE TWO: A SWEET KISS, A LING-
ERING TOUCH ... THAT'D DO.
(1719)

SWEPT ASIDE BY THE
ROILING TIDES OF YOUR EGO'S
PRIDE, I'M NULLIFIED.
(1712)

THE WHAT I KNEW. THE
WHO WAS YOU. WHERE? I DON'T CARE!
THE WHY? I STILL CRY.
(1685)

YOU'VE GOT IT ALL: CHARM,
BRAINS, BEAUTY. YET, SADLY, NOT
AN OUNCE OF MERCY.
(1678)

THE YOU I KNEW FLEW
AWAY, RATHER THAN STAY AND
FACE A FEW DARK DAYS.
(1666)

THAT SUN'LL STILL SHINE WHEN
WE PART. IT'LL ALL BE FINE … EX-
CEPT MY BROKEN HEART.
(1631)

I HAVE MY TRUE. YOU
DO, TOO. WE DON'T HAVE TO AG-
REE … JUST LET EACH BE.
(1612)

I'VE NEVER RUN FROM
CONFRONTATION AND THAT'S WHY
IT'S ME WITH NO ONE.
(1600)

I RAN AWAY TO-
DAY. HURTS TOO MUCH TO STAY: TOO
HIGH A PRICE TO PAY.
(1552)

THAT DAY. WE ALMOST
DIDN'T PART WAYS. IT'S WHERE MY MEM-
ORY STRAYS … AND STAYS.
(1505)

LOVE AIN'T NO NINE-TO-
FIVE. TO KEEP IT ALIVE COM-
MIT YOUR SOUL – OR ROLL!
(1416)

MY NAÏVETY PRE-
CLUDES COMPLETE CLARITY. SO-
DID YOU JUST DITCH ME?
(1401)

I WON'T FEEL – IT'S TOO
PAINFUL. I HAVE STOPPED THINKING.
IT MAKES MY BRAIN FULL.
(1257)

THE LOVE WE LOST ... IT'S
COSTLY. NOT SO YOU'D SEE, BUT
IN THE HEART OF ME.
(1247)

LIFELONG CONCERNS FOR
GOOD HEALTH FORCE BLUNT HONESTY:
YOU'RE TOXIC TO ME.
(1245)

I GAVE YOU MY BEST –
STILL FAILED YOUR TESTS. JUDGED LACKING,
YOU SENT ME PACKING.
(1221)

ALL THESE YEARS. I DON'T
FIGHT THE TEARS. I'M GLAD MISSING
YOU STILL MAKES ME SAD.
(1206)

CHASED YOU, GOT TOO CLOSE
TO THE SUN. SPURNED; CRASHED AND BURNED.
LESSON LEARNED – NOT FUN.
(1203)

TO MAINTAIN MY SAN-
ITY, I SUSTAIN THE VAN-
ITY YOU LOVE ME.
(1199)

CONFESS! IT'S PAST TIME
TO ADDRESS THE YOU THAT MADE
A MESS OF YOU. YES?
(1192)

I DIDN'T WANT TO DO
IT. YOU MADE ME NOT LOVE YOU.
HOW COULD THIS BE TRUE?
(1159)

YOU CAN'T BE OBJEC-
TIVE ABOUT ME. YOU TAKE IT
TOO PERSONALLY.
(1157)

TO YOUR CREDIT, YOU
SWORE YOU'D LEAVE. I JUST DIDN'T
BELIEVE WHEN YOU SAID IT.
(1145)

YOU RAINED ON MY PA-
RADE; SAW THOUGH MY SLEEK CHARADE …
ALL MY SCHEMES MISLAID.
(1116)

YOUR WEEPY SAD SONG'S
ALL WRONG. I DIDN'T CHEAT. YOU PLAIN
GOT BEAT. MOVE ALONG!
(1113)

I WON'T CONDONE YOUR
ATTEMPTS TO ATONE FOR BREAK-
ING MY HEART. WE'RE DONE.
(1090)

OLD TIME'S ENDING. NEW
ONE'S BEGUN. HOPES WE WERE SPEND-
ING WEREN'T THE RIGHT ONES.
(1062)

WE HAD A CHANCE – SLIM.
NOW IT'S GONE. WE IS DONE. NO MORE
ONE. JUST US – OR THEM.
(1060)

I'M STILL TRYING, BUT
GETTING NOWHERE. WHY ARE YOU
DENYING YOU CARE?
(1024)

MCKENNA – BRILLIANT:
CEASE PONDERING WHAT-IFS; FO-
CUS ON WHAT COULD BE.
(1015)

SWEET KYRA, CHILD OF
MY HEART – WHICH NEVER STOPS ACH-
ING WHEN WE'RE APART.
(1014)

VILE PAST WAYS BRED DARK
DAYS, BLACKER NIGHTS. I PRAY TO
ASSUAGE SELFISH FRIGHTS.
(1007)

THERE'S NO PLACE TO GO
OR HIDE. I'VE TRIED. YOU WON'T BE
DENIED! SATISFIED?
(1005)

HOPING TIME'S GONE! CRY-
ING TIME'S HERE! WE WON'T GET IT
DONE. NOW COMES THE FEAR.
(1000)

HI. YOU KNOW WHY I'M
NOT YOUR GUY, BUT NOT I. YOU
NEVER SAID WHY. BYE.
(998)

THEY SAY LOVE CURES ALL
OUR ILLS – EASY FOR THEM. THEY
DON'T PAY ALL YOUR BILLS.
(995)

I HAD A DREAM LONG
AGO – TO BE THERE, KNOW YOU,
CARE ... SO LONG AGO.
(987)

I SUMMON YOU AT
WILL. I STARE, YOU'RE THERE. NOT RARE,
IT GIVES ME A CHILL.
(948)

LET'S SEE. WITHOUT YOU
WHERE WOULD I BE? MOST LIKELY?
IN LOVE – HAPPILY.
(940)

YOUR PERSISTENCE IN
RESISTENCE DICTATES NEW STRAT-
EGIES FROM ME. THANKS.
(935)

I THOUGHT I KNEW YOU.
I DON'T EVEN KNOW ME. WHAT'S
TRUE? WHEN, WILL I, SEE?
(928)

FOR A BRIEF MOMENT
WE WERE ONE. THAT'S BEEN UNDONE.
NOW, HEARTACHE'S BEGUN.
(913)

I REMEMBER WHEN
I WAS HAPPY – MAINLY 'CAUSE
I DIDN'T KNOW YOU THEN.
(911)

TO ESCHEW CERTAIN
DOUBTS, PLUS PROBLEMS THAT ENSUE,
REFLECT ON "I DO."
(905)

MY WORST FEAR ISN'T DEATH.
IT'S THE DESPAIR BORN OF HOPE
THAT YOU MIGHT STILL CARE.
(903)

I DO WHAT I DO
TO NOT THINK OF YOU AND WHY
YOU DID WHAT YOU DID.
(899)

I DON'T KNOW HOW TO
LET GO. THE PAIN'S SO INTENSE
IT TURNS SENSE TO WOE.
(898)

MY HEAD'S SPINNING. I
CAN'T STOP GRINNING. AT LAST! YOU'VE
GONE! I CAN MOVE ON.
(897)

YOU HAVE TO KNOW: I'D
SELL MY SOUL FOR US TO BE
TOGETHER. DON'T GO.
(894)

SEE? BE HAPPY! YOUR
LEAVING RELEASED ME FROM SELF-
IMPOSED TYRANNY.
(873)

I FOUGHT THE GOOD FIGHT,
GOT IT MOSTLY RIGHT. LUCKY,
TOO, EXCEPT FOR YOU.
(853)

I THOUGHT NO ONE COULD
SURPRISE ME. THEN YOU SCREAMED YOUR
GOOD BYES. TEARY EYES.
(823)

I MISS THE CARESS
OF A STRONG LOVING HAND AND
A SOFT LINGERING KISS.
(815)

I RAN. YOU DIDN'T HAVE
TO. YOU KNEW WE WERE THROUGH SOON
AFTER WE BEGAN.
(814)

"JE NE REGRETE PAS"
WISH THAT WAS TRUE. I'M SICK
THAT I EVER MET YOU.
(804)

TELL ME WHY I CRY
OVER YOU, WHO DIDN'T EVEN
SAY GOOD-BYE: JUST FLEW!
(801)

WE FELL IN LOVE. IT
COULDN'T LAST. OUR FUTURE WAS HELD
HOSTAGE TO MY PAST.
(790)

YOU PLAY THE BLAME GAME
EVERYTIME, BUT IT'S NEV-
ER YOUR NAME, JUST MINE.
(788)

I THOUGHT I KNEW YOU,
COULD SEE RIGHT THROUGH. HOW NAÏVE
TO THINK YOU'D STAY TRUE.
(764)

I'LL FORGIVE, BUT CAN
NEVER FORGET. NOR WILL I
BE A HYPOCRITE.
(761)

"IT'S NOT YOU, IT'S ME."
MEANS: WE HAD OUR FUN. I'M DONE.
GOTTA RUN! SEE YA!
(759)

AN INCH OR A MILE,
A MISS IS A MISS. WE GOT
TO THAT INCH ... SO CLOSE.
(729)

WHICH DO I LOVE MOST?
THE YOU I *"KNEW"* WAS TRUE OR
THAT MEMORY'S GHOST?
(710)

THE MORE I THINK A-
BOUT IT, THE LESS I THINK YOU'RE
WORTH THINKING ABOUT.
(697)

EASY NOW WILL BE HARD
OVER TIME IF YOU'VE GOT TO
KEEP THE LIES GOING.
(680)

WHO, WHAT, WHERE, WHEN, MAY
VARY. WHY'S CONSTANT: WITH THE
MONEY, POWER'S YOURS.
(678)

I'M TOO WEARY TO
BE ANGRY, TOO BROKEN TO
BE MENDED. WE'RE THROUGH.
(677)

IN THE THROES OF MY
DESPAIR, I SEE YOU, TOUCH YOU.
IT'S JUST ... YOU'RE NOT THERE.
(670)

EXCLUDING YOUR DE-
MISE, NOTHING EXONER-
ATES YOU IN MY EYES.
(659)

TRY AS I MAY, WHAT
CAN I SAY? I RUE THE DAY
I PUSHED YOU AWAY.
(656)

COUPLES PASS ME BY.
I CRY, WONDERING: WHY SHOULDN'T
THAT BE YOU AND I?
(638)

THE EMPTINESS YOU
FEEL NOW'S NOTHING. WAIT 'TIL DES-
PERATION GRABS HOLD.
(635)

NO! WE CAN'T BE *"JUST
FRIENDS."* I WON'T FORGET WHAT WAS
EVEN THOUGH YOU HAVE.
(623)

I'M FINE, THANKS. YOU KNOW --
GOOD DAYS, BAD DAYS. HAVEN'T CRIED FOR
YOU IN, WHAT, EIGHT HOURS?
(609)

OUR SOCIAL CONTRACT'S
BROKEN BEYOND REDEMPTION.
NIHILISM'S GRINNING.
(608)

WHEN LOVE LEAVES, YOUR HEART
DIES, YOUR SOUL GRIEVES, YOUR MIND CRIES
"WHO BELIEVES SUCH LIES?"
(593)

THANKS! I HAD A GOOD
TIME TONIGHT. HOPE YOU DID TOO.
HAVE A GREAT LIFE. BYE!
(590)

I USED TO DANCE AND
SING. NOW I CRAWL AND CRY. YOU
KNOW THE REASON WHY.
(568)

CAN'T TELL YOU HOW MUCH
I'M GONNA MISS YOU. BE SURE
AND TAKE ALL YOUR STUFF.
(557)

MANY TIMES, I DIED.
EVEN MORE, I CRIED HOT TEARS.
BROUGHT BY LOVE DENIED.
(552)

MY BIGGEST REGRET?
THAT'S NOT LEAVING YOU TEN SE-
CONDS AFTER WE MET!
(551)

WITH AGE WISDOM? SUR-
PRISING HOW TENACIOUSLY
STUBBORNESS LINGERS.
(548)

THE TRAUMA OF YOUR
PARENTS FIGHTING, DIVORCING, NEV-
ER ABATES. MINE HASN'T.
(546)

INFATUATED,
I INSTANTLY IMAGINED
INTIMATE IDYLLS.
(542)

JUST CAN'T PULL MYSELF
TOGETHER: I'M STILL IN LOVE
WITH OUR MEMORIES.
(541)

THE BIGGEST WINNERS
OF THAT *"'TIL DEATH DO US PART"*
GAME ARE – DUH! – LAWYERS.
(531)

HUMANS! BEWARE! I'M
YOUR WORST NIGHTMARE. TOXIC – I
BELIEVE WE'RE EQUAL.
(496)

WHEN I SAID THOSE THINGS
DEMEANING YOU BE ASSURED –
IT WAS ON PURPOSE.
(495)

YOU'RE GONE! THAT DOESN'T
STOP ME FROM LOVING, WANTING
YOU. HOW COULD I NOT?
(474)

MY MIND TORMENTS MY
SOUL, OBSESSING OVER NOWS
RATHER THAN LATERS.
(450)

YOU PLUCK MY HEART STRINGS.
I DANCE TO YOUR TUNES. YOU CAN'T
KNOW WHAT PAIN THAT BRINGS.
(447)

I SURE HOPE THERE'S SOME-
THING I CAN DO TO KEEP YOU
FROM STICKING AROUND.
(438)

IF I COULD FIND IT
IN MY HEART TO FORGIVE YOU
I WOULD … BUT, I CAN'T.
(434)

*"THE FAULT'S (NOT) IN OUR
STARS" ... "WE HAVE MET THE EN-
EMY AND HE IS US".*
(429)

I'LL GET OVER YOU
IF, AND WHEN, THEY REASSEM-
BLE THE TITANIC.
(425)

I'M O.K. BY DAY,
BUT AT NIGHT OUR MEMORIES
GUSH OUT WITH MY TEARS.
(423)

YOU DON'T MISS MUCH, SAVE
THAT YOU CAN'T SEE OR FEEL THE
LOVE SURROUNDING YOU.
(413)

I DIDN'T SAY *"I LOVE
YOU"* ENOUGH, TOOK YOU FOR GRANTED.
I WOULD HAVE LEFT, TOO.
(403)

A LIFE'S LAMENT: NO-
ONE'S EVER UTTERED THIS: *"YOU
BELONG HERE WITH ME."*
(380)

MY HEART TELLS ME TO
LOVE YOU. MY HEAD SCREAMS *"GET THE
HELL OUT!"* THINK I'LL STAY.
(379)

WHEN ALL'S SAID AND DONE
WE'VE GOT TO LIVE WITH OURSELVES.
SO … HOW YOU DOIN'?
(362)

DESPAIRING OF SIN-
CERE KINDNESS, I FIND REFUGE
IN STARK SOLITUDE.
(358)

SHUNNING LIGHT, MINE'S A
SHADOW WORLD OF UNFULFILLED
HOPES AND SHATTERED DREAMS.
(357)

KNOWING THAT WHAT SHOULD
BE WON'T, MY HEART HURTS WITH EV-
ERY THOUGHT OF YOU.
(356)

THOUGHTS OF YOU, HEIRLOOMS
OF HAPPINESS, BACKLIGHT MY
MIND'S BROODING PRESENT.
(287)

YOU TOOK THE WE THAT
WAS US AND HACKED OUT DOUR
SINGULARITIES.
(286)

MEMORIES OF US
ENDURE ALTHOUGH WE ARE MINDS,
AND OCEANS, APART.
(207)

MY NEW FRIENDS – HEARTACHE
AND GLOOM – ACTIVELY SUSTAIN
ME SINCE YOU WALKED OUT.
(183)

MASSIVE WALLS OF ICE
ON STERILE WASTELANDS ENSHROUD
MY HEART SINCE YOU FLED.
(81)

BOOK FOUR

SELF AWARENESS

SELF-IMAGE BROUGHT LOW,
IF REGAINED, WON'T ATTAIN IT'S
PRE-LOSS GLOSS AND GLOW.
(2107)

CENSURE WE ENDURE
FROM *"WELL MEANT"* COMMENTS WON'T IN-
URE US FROM SELF DOUBT.
(2106)

WHILE TAKING A CUE
FROM HAIKU, I EXPRESS MY
TRUE THROUGH SENRYU.
(2102)

MY MIND SEES WHAT MY
SOUL FEELS. MY HEART SINGS THESE, MY
REALITIES. ME.
(2088)

ROUGH BRED, WIDELY READ,
SCAMMING -- TO STAY TWO STEPS A-
HEAD OF GETTING DEAD.
(2079)

WAIT? SEE? NOT FOR ME:
BRAIN CHEMISTRY SAYS NO TO
SLOW. GOTTA MOVE, GO!
(2077)

I SHOUT. RANT. RAVE. GOT
TO GET IT OUT, FEARFUL THAT,
IF NOT, IT'S MY GRAVE.
(2076)

EFFUSIVE PRAISE TENDS
TO RAISE CAUTION'S GATE, LETTING
DOUBTS PROLIFERATE.
(2075)

MY GLORY DAYS BE-
HIND ME, SOON WORRY'S WAYS WILL
FIND ME. I'M WORTHY.
(2073)

MY THUNDER IS WORSE
THAN HELL'S. IT'LL TEAR YOU ASUN-
DER. I'LL LIVE TO TELL.
(2071)

VANITY, EGO'S
SELF-INDUCED CALAMITY,
DENIES CLARITY.
(2068)

DESPITE ALL THAT I'VE
SAID, I MIGHT NOT BE QUITE RIGHT
IN MY HEAD … DON'T TREAD.
(2062)

TOO FEW WEAR THEIR HEARTS
AS A SLEEVE. THOSE OF US WHO
DO, CANNOT DECEIVE.
(2059)

REALITY ISN'T
SHARED. HOW I SEE WHAT I SEE –
ME – CAN'T BE COMPARED.
(2055)

AS I CROSS A LINE,
AGAIN, I REMIND ME, A-
GAIN, SO GOES MANKIND.
(2054)

PSYCHIC RESIDUE
FROM BATTLES WE DO TAINTS OUR
LIFE VIEW. CLEANSE. RE-NEW.
(2051)

MY END'S NEARER. SEIZED
BY TERROR, I STARE IN A
MIRROR: BLAME'S CLEARER.
(2044)

NOT CONTENT TO AC-
CEPT *"FATE"*, I DO MY BEST TO
AGITATE ... I GRATE.
(2043)

DOING'S THROUGH. NEEDING'S
NEW. YOUNG ME KNEW, CONFIDENT.
THIS ME, HASN'T A CLUE.
(2041)

I'M THE MEANS TO MY
ENDS, NO GO-BETWEENS, NO MAK-
ING AMENDS. I'LL WIN.
(2040)

QUOTIDIAN CHORES,
ROUTINE BORES, TAKE UP MOST OF
OUR DAY. THAT'S LIFE'S WAY.
(2038)

BOOM DAYS DONE, GRAYING
BEGUN, I SEEK MEANING AS
MY TIME ENDS ITS RUN.
(2037)

IF YEARNING WAS LEARN-
ING, I'D BE EARNING A B.
A. EVERY DAY.
(2015)

NOT PROGRESSIVE, NOT
CONSERVATIVE, I'M MIDA-
TIVE: STRADDLING CENTER.
(2004)

I WRITE THE WAY I
DO TO SHOCK YOU INTO SEE-
ING ... WITHOUT THINKING!
(2003)

THE ME I LET YOU
SEE IS A SHADOW OF THE
ME I KNOW I AM.
(2002)

ME? NOT NICE. I DO
WHAT I NEED TO, DON'T THINK TWICE.
BEST HEED THIS ADVICE.
(2001)

INSIDE MY OUT? I
TREMBLE, SHAKE, FULL OF DOUBT. OUT-
SIDE MY IN? FAKE GRIN.
(1998)

MY OLD AGE SHOWS A
LATENT RAGE FOR DUE PROCESS.
LET CHAOS PROGRESS!
(1987)

ACQUIRING WEALTH TEACH-
ES DISTRUST AND STEALTH, RARELY
GENEROSITY.
(1984)

MELANCHOLY'S MY
NAME; REGRET MY SHAME. ME FIRST,
ALWAYS, WAS MY GAME.
(1983)

I DON'T TELL LIES, JUST
ALIBIS; *MOSTLY* TRUE WITH
A FEW FACTS DISGUISED.
(1980)

I AM THE BLINDING
LIGHT THAT ILLUMINATES MY
FRIGHT. TOO SCARY, RIGHT?
(1975)

LOVERS! HERE IS LOVE'S
GREATEST GIFT: GIVING, NOT RE-
CEIVING. THAT'S LIVING.
(1972)

I AM NOT, WOULD NOT,
COULD NOT, SHOULD NOT, WILL NOT BE
ANYONE BUT ME.
(1966)

MOST APPEAR TO BE *"GOOD."*
BUT, WHAT WOULD THEY DO IF IT
WAS *"THEM OR US"*? GUESS.
(1962)

CLOWNISH, KAFKAESQUE,
MY LIFE'S AN ED POE BURLESQUE –
AND FUNNY IT'S NOT.
(1959)

BUT FOR A TURNING
HERE, A YEARNING THERE, FATE WOULD
HAVE LED EACH TO ... WHERE?
(1944)

ANTICIPATION'S
JOYS AREN'T DIMINISHED BY RE-
ALITY'S TARNISH.
(1943)

I ATTAINED CRITI-
CAL MASS AT TEN. SINCE THEN, IT'S
BEEN A WAITING GAME.
(1939)

CONSEQUENCES: SOME
WILL SPARE YOU BY MILES, SOME WILL
SNARE YOU BY INCHES.
(1932)

WHEN I SEE THE ME
I'VE COME TO BE, HONESTLY,
IT FLABBERGASTS ME.
(1931)

THE TOLL YOU EXACT
FROM BODY AND MIND IS BEST
DEFINED AS ... WORTH IT.
(1929)

ALL MY LIFE I'VE BEEN
ON CALL, STANDING BY, WATCHING –
A FLY ON THE WALL.
(1926)

WHEN SILENT SCREAMS ARE
HEARD, THAT PAIN'S SUFFERING CAN'T
BE CALMED BY JUST WORDS.
(1913)

NOT DECORATING
MEANS NOTHING TO TAKE DOWN, MORE
TIME TO GRUMP AND FROWN.
(1902)

BEEN STUCK IN REVERSE
FOR YEARS – LIKELY 'CAUSE I FEAR
TO ADDRESS MY FEARS.
(1899)

HEADING SOMEWHERE, FOR-
GETTING WHY I'M THERE, FRAYS
MY NERVES AND GRAYS MY HAIR.
(1896)

INCIPIENT, IN-
CREMENTAL INSANITY
IS INSIDIOUS.
(1891)

A FRAGILE MIND PRO-
JECTS *"I'M FINE"* TO DEFLECT IT'S
(IMAGINED?) DECLINE.
(1890)

NOT ONE TO HIDE, I'LL
SAY WHAT'S INSIDE: I OPEN
MY MOUTH – THINGS GO SOUTH.
(1889)

I'VE NEVER NEEDED TO
BE THE BEST – JUST SATISFY
MYSELF IN LIFE'S TESTS.
(1884)

TO KNOW *THE* WAY, I
MUST GO MY WAY – NOT SLOW FOR
WHAT OTHERS MAY SAY.
(1874)

WE ALL KNOW OUR TRUE,
BUT TOO FEW ADMIT THEY DO
TO THEMSELVES. IT'S TIME.
(1873)

YOU DID ME DIRT. IT
SURELY HURT. I WON'T JUDGE, BUT
WILL CARRY A GRUDGE.
(1864)

CONTEMPT LIBER-
ATES ME. EXEMPT FROM FEELINGS
I'M, BY DEGREES, FREE.
(1862)

FUNCTIONAL INSAN-
ITY IS MY PLEA. SO, DON'T
LABEL ME CRAZY.
(1861)

WHO AM I? WE SPEND
OUR LIVES SEEKING TRUTH ONLY
WE CAN VERIFY.
(1858)

A PRISONER OF
MY THOUGHTS, I TRY TO ESCAPE,
BUT ALWAYS GET CAUGHT.
(1857)

MOST CONFLICT'S BETWEEN
ME AND MY CONSCIENCE GO MY
WAY. WHAT CAN I SAY?
(1856)

THE LATEST LAMENT
OF MY SELF-PITY SPREE: *"HOW
CAN THEY NOT GET ME?"*
(1847)

THE INTRICACY,
DELICACY OF HEARTACHE,
PARALYZES ME.
(1846)

I WANT NOT TO WANT.
I NEED NOT TO NEED. ABSENT
THESE – I WANT, I NEED!
(1845)

OLD HURTS BURIED DEEP
CAUSE MANY TO CRY, NOT KNOW-
ING WHY … BUT, I KNOW.
(1844)

ALL I KNOW SLOWLY
ERODES AS AGING ISSUES
ITS MANDATE: CORRODE!
(1836)

WE KNOW WHERE WE'D LIKE
TO GO. THE WAY CONFUSES,
STIRS UP UNDERTOW.
(1834)

CONCENTRATING ON
HATING MAKES MY FEARS ABATE.
I'M SAFER ... WORKS GREAT!
(1831)

WITH NO FAITH IN HU-
MANITY, I PRESERVE MY
SANITY. WHAT FOR?
(1829)

I HOLD MY NOSE AND
FLICK MY THUMBS AT SOCIE-
TY'S FAUX DECORUMS.
(1825)

THE WORLD I KNEW HAS
GONE ASKEW. TOO SET, TOO OLD,
I REFUTE THIS NEW.
(1824)

I'VE A CONNECTION
TO REALITY. IT'S A
FINE LINE YOU CAN'T SEE.
(1818)

*"DON'T DO AS I DO,
DO AS I SAY"*: THE WAY I
WAS RAISED – TO OBEY.
(1817)

I'M NOT POSSESSED OF
SUFFICIENT IMAGINA –
TION TO PONDER TRUTHS.
(1816)

IT'S NOT FATE THAT HOLDS
SWAY. IT'S US. WE JUST CAN'T GET
OUT OF OUR OWN WAY.
(1814)

AFTER COFFEE I
ASK ME *"WHAT'LL I DO TODAY?"*
SELF SAYS *"WAIT AND SEE."*
(1811)

MY BANE OF EXIS-
TENCE IS AN ARCANE INSIS-
TANCE ON BEING ME.
(1807)

FORTIFIED BY UN-
RELENTING PRIDE, I DON'T DWELL
ON WHAT'S DIED INSIDE.
(1802)

AGING'S MOLLIFIED
ME. I OOZE SENTIMENTAL-
ITY – LUCKILY.
(1801)

TENSION'S AC, FREE
FLOWING FROM MIND TO MOUTH TO
MIND. NO WIRES REQUIRED.
(1798)

THE MORE I SEE THE
MORE I CRY. THE MORE I CRY
THE MORE I SCREAM WHY?
(1789)

I FORTHWITH DECREE
I'M DONE TAKING ME SERI-
OUSLY ... TOO HEAVY.
(1786)

OBLIVIOUS TO
ALL THINGS OBVIOUS, I'M A
CLOWN IN LIFE'S CIRCUS.
(1785)

THE LAST THING I WANT?
THE FIRST THING I NEED? LET GO
OF MY PAST ... BE FREED.
(1783)

SUSPICIOUS, ANXIOUS,
NERVOUS, WITTY, I'M PERFECT-
LY GREGARIOUS.
(1781)

TRACES OF REMORSE
LEAK FROM MY EYES, WHEN I RE-
CALL MY ALIBIS.
(1779)

HOSTAGE TO A SAV-
AGE PRIDE, I'M SLOWLY DISIN-
TEGRATING INSIDE.
(1774)

YOU'VE BEATEN ME AT
EVERY TURN. I SMILE OUT-
SIDE, BUT INSIDE, I BURN.
(1752)

REGRET COMPOUNDS, OFF-
SET, IN QUIET MOMENTS, WHEN
HAPPINESS ABOUNDS.
(1751)

STAR-CROSSED, TOSSED ADRIFT
BY LIFE'S STORMY SEA, I'M LOST
AND CANNOT SWIM FREE.
(1747)

PROGRESS REPORT: *"WHO
AM I? WHERE AM I GOING?
IS IT WORTH KNOWING?"*
(1743)

I'M INCLINED TO RE-
DESIGN YOUR JAW LINE. ONE THING
RESTRAINS ME -- JAIL TIME.
(1717)

I'VE SEEN THINGS NO ONE
SHOULD SEE. I'VE BEEN PLACES NO
ONE SHOULD BE. SADLY.
(1716)

WHATEVER *'IN'* MEANS
I'VE NEVER BEEN THERE, JUST
SORTA IN-BETWEEN.
(1713)

I FIGHT WITH MY BRAIN.
IT'S QUITE NECESSARY. IF
NOT, I'D BE INSANE.
(1710)

TRUTH BE TOLD (RARELY),
I'M NOT SOLD ON VERACI-
TY AS POLICY.
(1703)

YOU KNOW WHAT? IT'S WAY
PAST TIME FOR ME TO CLIMB OUT
OF MY RUT! BUT ... HOW?
(1690)

THE ONE TO BLAME FOR
MY FAME – OR SHAME – IS, ALWAYS
NEAR-BY. SURPRISE!
(1657)

DO I RUN? STAY AND
FIGHT? PLEASE! SOMEONE TELL ME WHAT'S
RIGHT ... I'VE COME UNDONE.
(1653)

OUTSIDE THE *"IN"* CROWD,
I'VE GAINED PERSPECTIVE: HAPPI-
NESS IS ELECTIVE.
(1650)

AFRAID TO LET THE
WORLD SEE, THE REAL ME, I ACT
THE FOOL. BREEZILY.
(1649)

I LASSO THE WIND,
I CHASE RAINBOWS: I TWIST, TURN,
BEND – BUT WON'T GIVE IN.
(1647)

CONTEMPLATING CAN
BE MOTIVATING OR IN-
CAPACITATING.
(1637)

THE SURE IN ME IS
OVERWHELMED BY UNCERTAIN-
TY. I TREAD LIGHTLY.
(1636)

WITH EACH STROKE OF MY
PEN, I DEFY LIFE DENY-
ING OBLIVION.
(1635)

MY WHISPERED PRAYERS ARE
HOWLS INTO THE VOID. IS THERE
ANYONE WHO CARES?
(1634)

MAN'S WAYS, EVER AS-
KEW, SIMPLY STATED, ARE FEW: *"ME
FIRST, THEN, MAYBE, YOU."*
(1632)

MOST OF US KNOW WHAT
WE SHOULD DO, BUT LACK MORAL
CALM TO FOLLOW THROUGH.
(1630)

YOU'RE THE ME I WANT
TO BE … I LACK YOUR SUBTLE-
TY AND CLARITY.
(1627)

I AIN'T GONNA SPIN
IT. I'M IN IT TO WIN IT.
LOSIN'S TOO BRUISIN'.
(1610)

I'M NUMBING DAILY,
BECOMING A NON-ENTI-
TY – FOR MY SAFETY.
(1604)

I FEED MY ILLUS-
IONS. WHEN THEY SEEM REAL, I DON'T
REVEAL HOW I FEEL.
(1599)

THERE'LL COME A DAY, SOON,
WHEN WE ALL HAVE TO PAY FOR
WHAT WE DO – AND SAY.
(1598)

IN MY PRIME I'D DREAM
OF GAIN AND CLIMB. AGED, I SCHEME
TO RETAIN LOST TIME.
(1597)

I LOVED. LOST. TRIED A-
GAIN. SAME. WE GET BURNED, WE LEARN.
I'M OUT OF THAT GAME.
(1592)

I HAVE A NIGHTMARE,
WHERE MANKIND'S IN DEEP DESPAIR –
THERE'S NO ONE TO HATE.
(1590)

IF OTHERS COULD SEE
WHAT I DO TO ME, THEY'D QUES-
TION MY SANITY.
(1586)

I'VE HAD SUNSHINE AND
LOTS OF RAIN. THEY TAUGHT ME TO
OWN MINE – TO MY GAIN.
(1578)

THERE'S NO ONE TO BLAME
FOR ME – BUT ME! I GOT LIFE
WRONG. WOULDN'T SEE – SADLY.
(1573)

I LEFT THE BEST OF
ME TO FIND TRUE DESTINY.
STILL GROPING BLINDLY.
(1572)

SOME INSIST THEIR BI-
OGRAPHY BE HAGIOG-
RAPHY. NEVER ME.
(1566)

WHEN I STUMBLE OR
FALL, I STAGGER OR CRAWL 'TIL
I'M UP, STANDING TALL.
(1564)

FANTASY HAS ITS
GRIP ON ME. REALITY
FADES OUT READILY.
(1557)

FOR ME INTROSPEC-
TION ISN'T MERE REFLECTION. IT'S
LIFE'S PHILOSOPHY.
(1548)

I BOUGHT INTO *"WE'RE
ALL EQUAL."* ALL IT GOT ME
WAS ITS SEQUEL: NOT!
(1547)

MY TROUBLES ARE HERE –
STILL! THEIR SOLUTION'S NIL. FAIL-
URE'S A BITTER PILL.
(1508)

HAD IT. LOST IT. CAN'T
GET ON TRACK. PRAYIN', ONE DAY,
TO FIND A WAY BACK.
(1507)

AS A YOUTH, I STAYED
INSIDE THE LINES. LONG OF TOOTH,
I ABHOR CONFINES.
(1506)

I'M TIPSY, TEETER-
ING; ON THE BRINK OF BLANKED OUT
NON-THINK: PSYCHO-Y.
(1500)

EACH DAY IT GETS WORSE.
WONDER HOW MUCH LONGER? HARD
TO SAY. PRAY. PONDER.
(1498)

CAN'T KNOW WHAT'S GOOD FOR
ME, 'TIL I KNOW WHAT'S NOT GOOD
FOR ME. AIN'T EASY.
(1497)

WITH AGE CAME A DREAD
OF STAYING *"AHEAD."* INSTEAD
I TRY TO *"LOAD SHED."*
(1496)

I'M ONE-EIGHTY OUT
TO MOST VIEWS ON WHAT LIFE'S A-
BOUT: IT'S HEAR – NOT SHOUT.
(1495)

WITH NO GIVE AND TAKE,
HEAVY ON BOTH ENDS, THE CEN-
TER WON'T BEND – JUST BREAK!
(1494)

MY HEART'S ELASTIC
WITH LOTS OF GIVE: EASIER
TO LIVE – AND FORGIVE.
(1493)

MINUS AN END GAME
I'VE LIVED LIFE FRAME TO FRAME: RISK-
Y, QUIRKY, NOT TAME.
(1492)

I HAVE NOUGHT, BUT WHAT
LABOR HATH BROUGHT, NOR HAVE I
SOUGHT A PENNY MORE.
(1490)

I'M GOOD AT CONCEAL-
ING, NEVER REVEALING, MY
FEELINGS. TRUTH'S PAINFUL.
(1485)

IN IT, OF IT, TRY-
ING TO RISE ABOVE IT: STILL –
I YEARN TO LOVE LIFE.
(1483)

MY DEFAULT SETTING'S
SELFISHNESS. WHAT'S IT FOR MOST
OTHERS? TAKE A GUESS.
(1481)

O.K. SO I KNOW
I DON'T KNOW ANYTHING: THIS
MAKES ME *"IN THE KNOW."*
(1479)

I TOOK IT PAST YOUR
LIMIT … LOST. WHO KNOWS WHY? MY
GUESS – NEEDED TO WIN IT.
(1478)

TOSSED AROUND, NOT YET
FOUND, ADRIFT ON THE SEA OF
TRYING TO FIND ME.
(1476)

I WANTED TO CALL. NO
GUTS, THAT'S ALL. YOU O.K.? I'LL
TRY AGAIN … SOMEDAY.
(1472)

I'M TRAPPED IN MY MIND.
SCARED I MIGHT FIND WHAT I THINK
I MIGHT KNOW CAN'T BE SO.
(1468)

NOT CHOOSING TO, BUT
LOSING TO, NEGATIVI-
TY. WHO'S THE REAL ME?
(1465)

NEVER A WILD CHILD;
I WAS CALM, COMPOSED, RARELY
RILED – AND BARELY SMILED.
(1461)

STEP OUTSIDE YOUR SKIN;
SEE YOU AS OTHERS DO. JUST
MIGHT NOT WANT BACK IN.
(1460)

INNER PEACE REQUIRES
CONFIDENCE. CAN'T BE HAD IF
ONE SITS ON THE FENCE.
(1459)

I AM NOT WHO YOU
THINK I AM. I AM WHO I
KNOW I AM. SO … SCRAM!
(1456)

THE SUM OF MY FEARS
IS STARING IN MIRRORS AND
FACING ALL THOSE YEARS.
(1455)

MY TIME FOR LOVE'S GONE
BY. I AIMED TOO HIGH, WOULDN'T SEE
IT'S TOO LATE FOR ME.
(1452)

I'M NO ONE'S KEEPER,
ONLY A JUMP START, A LEAP-
ER FROM HEART TO HEART.
(1450)

I HAVE A PLACE. IT'S
WHERE I GO WHEN I CAN'T FACE
ALL THE THINGS I KNOW.
(1449)

I SCREAM MY SOLI-
TUDE TO THE WIND. IT WHISPERS
"YOU'RE NOT ALONE FRIEND."
(1447)

IRONY REQUIRES
FINESSE, ESCHEWS LARGESSE AND
AND LEAVES EGOS NO REST.
(1445)

I'M IN SHADOW, A
HALF-LIFE FEW KNOW; AN IN-BE-
TWEEN WHERE LOST SOULS GO.
(1444)

I SOARED ON WINGS OF
YOUTH, SKY HIGH. GRAYER, GROUNDED,
JUST WANNA TO GET BY.
(1439)

I'VE BEEN THERE. SOMEWHERE
BETWEEN FEAR AND CRYING HOPE
SNEAKS AWAY, SIGHING.
(1437)

IN THE DARK OF MY
MIND THOUGHTS I CONSIGNED TO HOPE
BEGAN TO FIND LIGHT.
(1432)

I KNOW WHAT I WANT
TO SAY, BUT WHEN I DO IT
DOESN'T COME OUT THAT WAY.
(1430)

TO FUNCTION GOTTA
HAVE GUMPTION. I GOT, UM – NONE!
GOT TO GO FIND SOME.
(1426)

THE PROCESS IS SLOW,
BUT THOROUGH: PICK YOURSELF UP;
AIM; MOVE FEET; REPEAT.
(1422)

I'M REJECTED, EJECTED –
THUS DISCONNECTED – FROM SOCI-
ETY. I BLAME ME.
(1410)

I DON'T KNOW SLOW. CAN'T
DO ANYTHING BUT "GO!" IF
NOT, I'LL GET CAUGHT. BYE!
(1405)

AN OBSESSION YOU'LL
FAIL ENSURES THAT THE SLIGHTEST
PUFF WILL FLUFF YOUR SAIL.
(1400)

I PRETEND, A LOT,
TO BE WHAT I'M NOT. IN THE
END IT'S STILL ME – CAUGHT.
(1397)

I PEEKED AT TOMOR-
ROW. IT'S FULL OF SORROW. SO,
SOMEHOW, ENJOY NOW.
(1396)

I DON'T TAKE AGEING
IN STRIDE. I WON'T LET'EM PUNCH
MY TICKET TO RIDE.
(1395)

LUCKILY, I WAS
NEVER DECEIVED BY THE PRE-
TENSE THAT LIFE MAKES SENSE.
(1385)

I DON'T NEED TO BE
"LIKED" OR WELL-KNOWN, JUST LEFT A-
LONE, FREE, FINDING ME.
(1383)

WHAT I LEARNED IN SCHOOL
MADE ME LIFE'S FOOL: I BOUGHT IN-
TO THE *"GOLDEN RULE."*
(1373)

THE WORST PART OF LONE-
LINESS IS ONLY-NESS. I'M
A MESS. ONE AIN'T FUN.
(1368)

I HAVEN'T LOST *"IT."* IT'S
JUST THAT, AT TIMES, I HAVE SOME
PROBLEMS FINDING *"IT."*
(1367)

IN MY DAY, I HAD
PLENTY TO SAY. AGED. SPENT. MOST-
LY SILENT ... MOSTLY.
(1365)

WITH NO YEN TO BE
"IN", I'M TO THE RIGHT OF ZEN:
SPARTAN'S MY BIG WIN.
(1364)

EACH DAY MY TO-DO
LIST LENGTHENS. EACH NIGHT MY WILL
TO PUT-OFF STRENGTHENS.
(1362)

WHO YOU SEE ISN'T ME.
I FIXATED ON WANNA BE,
SHUNNED REALITY.
(1359)

WISH YOU COULD BUT SEE
THE WHO I'D CHOOSE TO BE – IF
I COULD CONTROL ME.
(1357)

THOUGHT I KNEW ME. NOT
TRUE. HOW COULD I AND STILL DO
HALF THE THINGS I DO?
(1356)

ANONIMITY
IS AVOIDANCE THERAPY:
THEN THEY CAN'T HURT ME.
(1353)

I SPENT MY PRIME WAST-
ING TIME, COUNTING ON TOMOR-
ROW – TO MY SORROW.
(1350)

WITH MOTIVATION
LACKING, ENNUI'S ATTACK-
ING. I'M SLACKING OFF.
(1347)

WIN OR LOSE, IT'S ALL
DOWN TO TIMING – WE CAN'T CHOOSE
WHEN OUR CLOCK'S CHIMING.
(1343)

LONG TIME BEEN PRAYING
TO FIND A CRACK IN THESE CLOUDS
THAT DEFINE MY LIFE.
(1342)

I WOULDN'T SEE. BLAME ME.
MY LIFE'S A LIE. I THOUGHT I
WAS NEVER WRONG. WHY?
(1337)

MY ART'S NOT MEANT TO
BE VIEWED OR HEARD. IT'S BEAUTY
IS THOUGHTS, WELL PLACED: WORDS.
(1336)

LOOK! MY LIFE'S AN O-
PEN BOOK. SO, WHAT IF THERE'S ON-
LY ONE PAGE -- OUTRAGE?
(1334)

MY PROBLEM IS I
SEE PROBLEMS, BEFORE PROBLEMS
REVEAL. SURREAL!
(1333)

WITH NO SOCIAL FIL-
TER, I'M AKILTER. LACKING
GUILE, I TEND TO RILE.
(1331)

IF YOU ASK ME – WHICH
YOU'LL REGRET – I'LL TELL YOU WHAT
I THINK. PLACE YOUR BET!
(1330)

I DO WHAT I DO
'CAUSE IT FEELS LIKE WHAT I NEED –
PLAIN 'OLE EGO FEED.
(1329)

IN MY PRIME, MY DREAM
WAS GAIN AND CLIMB. AGED, I SCHEME
TO RETAIN LOST TIME.
(1327)

A BALLOON WITH NO
AIR, I'M DEFLATED, BARELY THERE.
DOES ANYONE CARE?
(1324)

MY TALE'S FRAUGHT WITH WOE.
I'M ASSAILED, WHERE ERE I GO.
WHY? MY EGO'S FRAIL.
(1316)

LONG AN OUTLIER,
BEYOND THE PALE, I'M NO DE-
NIER: I WON'T BALE!
(1312)

I'VE BEGUN TO COME
UNDONE. AS THE BODY FAILS,
THE MIND WAILS *"NO FUN!"*
(1307)

I DON'T, AND WON'T, AL-
WAYS AGREE, BUT I ACCEPT
LIFE AS IT FINDS ME.
(1302)

MADE A WISH. GOT ALL
I ASKED FOR. WON'T BE MAKING
WISHES ANYMORE.
(1295)

I'M NO WILD ONE. GOT
NO GAME. DON'T CRAVE ATTENTION,
WON'T GO HUNTING FAME.
(1290)

FUMBLING BY DAY, TUM-
BLING AT NIGHT, CAN'T SAY I'VE A-
DAPTED TO THIS WORLD'S WAYS.
(1287)

TRAPPED BY MY MIND: SCARED
I MIGHT FIND WHAT I THINK I
KNOW CANNOT BE SO.
(1285)

AS I UNRAVEL
MY SHROUD OF MEMORY, EACH
THREAD TEACHES ME ME.
(1284)

I'M THE FLAMING PYRE
OF MY VANITY! EGO'S
FIRE BURNS WITHIN ME.
(1277)

FOR BETTER, OR WORSE,
I'VE GOT A GIFT FOR VERSE: COMIC,
LOGIC, RUSTIC, TERSE.
(1272)

RAPID REPARTEE
ISN'T MY FORTÉ. SARCASM WITH
BITE IS MY ENTRÉE.
(1266)

A DEVOUT RECLUSE,
I RARELY GO OUT. THAT MAKES
ME, NO DOUBT, OBTUSE.
(1262)

MY BRAIN'S SUBSONIC
YET SERVES ME AS WELL AS ALL
THINGS ELECTRONIC.
(1261)

THE RESTRAINTS OF CON-
STRAINTS FOIL ME. I NEED TO
UNWIND, BE UNREFINED.
(1254)

GOT NO MONEY OR FAME.
NO ONE KNOWS MY NAME. NOT ALL
SHAME, THOUGH: I GOT GAME!
(1252)

CURIOUSITY
DRYS WHEN EXPECTATIONS DIE.
FOR BOTH, FEAR'S THE WHY.
(1242)

A CONFIRMED MISAN-
THROPE, I'M NOT DEVOID OF HOPE …
'THOUGH IT'S A VAGUE GROPE.
(1241)

PRIDE'S MY DARK SIDE. I
HIDE BEHIND ITS ARMOR, BLIND
TO TRUTHS I'VE DENIED.
(1239)

I SEEK TO SUSPEND
BELIEF, HOPING TO BRING RE-
LIEF FROM MY THOUGHTS … NOT!
(1238)

MORE AND MORE, IT SEEMS
MY LIFE'S A NIGHTMARE SCHEME. I
AM BECOME MUNCH'S *"SCREAM."*
(1237)

NEEDED TO BE NEAT AND
TIDY – YOUTHFUL SINS. AGED. FO-
CUSED. MAKING AMENDS.
(1234)

OBSCURE, DEMURE, I
LIVE ON THE SLY, LEARNING
AS OTHERS FLY BY.
(1231)

PORTIONS OF MY PER--
SONALITY ARE SERVED HOT
WITH SPICY PASSION.
(1225)

HIDDEN BEHIND A
CLOWN'S FACE OF GAB AND GLAM, NO
ONE KNOWS WHO I AM.
(1220)

I BLUSH AT OUR RUSH
TO MISCONSTRUE FALSE AS TRUE.
WHEN ALL'S TRUE, WHAT'S TRUE?
(1215)

LACKING INTERNAL
CENSORSHIP, I'M ALWAYS PRONE
TO LIP SLIPS … NOT HIP.
(1214)

I'VE BEEN MISSING MY-
SELF OF LATE. HOW DID I EX-
CEED MY USE-BY DATE?
(1207)

A MASTER OF DIS-
GUISE, I HIDE MY BROKEN HEART
BEHIND TWINKLING EYES.
(1205)

THE WAY I WAS BACK
THEN? WELL … NEVER BE LIKE THAT
AGAIN. GOTTA GRIN.
(1202)

I PRETENDED TO KNOW
MORE THAN I KNOW … CAN'T STAND THE
TASTE OF EATING CROW.
(1201)

MOTTLED SKIN, GRAY HAIR
THIN, MEMORIES OF BEGIN-
INGS SPINNING – TIME WINS.
(1198)

I DID IT MY WAY –
DANCED TO MY TUNE. THAT PIPER'S
PAYDAY COMES DUE SOON.
(1197)

I'VE PLACED MY WELFARE
ON DEFERAL HEEDING MY
HEART'S REFERRAL – LOVE.
(1195)

MY MIND REDACTS AS
IT REACTS TO LIFE'S FACTS: TOO
MUCH SELF-CENSORSHIP.
(1191)

I NEED TO BE LOVED,
WANTED. MY LIFE'S BEEN HAUNTED BY THE
LIMITS I EXCEED.
(1185)

A YOUNG, SPONGY QUICK
STUDY, I'M NOW AN AGED, HARD-
HEADED FUDDY-DUDDY.
(1168)

YEARS OF ANGER AND
RAGE DO NOTHING TO ASSUAGE
MY CRIPPLING DESPAIR.
(1166)

LOST. NEVER FOUND. I
WANDER AROUND FOR DAYS IN
A GRAY HAZE. OH WELL.
(1164)

IN ORDER TO EX-
TEND OUR LIFE'S LEASE, YEARS-LONG WRONG
HABITS HAVE TO CEASE.
(1161)

ARTFUL DECEIT'S NOT
COMPLETE WITHOUT CHARMING MAN-
NERS AND SELF-CONCEIT.
(1160)

I LIKE MY SITU-
ATION. THE LESS CONTACT, THE
LESS CONFRONTATION.
(1155)

I LOST IT TODAY.
TOTAL BERZERK. FIGHTING BACK
COSTS. TOO MUCH HARD WORK.
(1153)

COMPLICATIONS A-
RISE WHEN, BIG SURPRISE, WE CAN'T
RECALL ALL OUR LIES.
(1152)

MY LIFE PLAN? PREPARE
FOR THE WORST, PRAY FOR THE BEST.
I'LL BE CURSED -- OR BLESSED.
(1101)

I DID WHAT I THOUGHT
WAS RIGHT. GOOD THING NO ONE EV-
ER PAID ME TO THINK.
(1099)

FALLIBLE, FLAWED, I'M
TOTALLY IN THRALL TO YOU,
OVERWHELMED AND AWED.
(1095)

MY SANITY COMES,
THEN GOES -- BUT, WHO KNOWS, MAYBE
I'VE BEEN GAMING ME.
(1076)

I KNOW YOU DON'T KNOW
ALL I KNOW ABOUT YOU. KNOW
THIS: YOU SHOULD FEAR ME.
(1070)

I'M NOT WORTHY OF
LOVE. NEVER HAVE BEEN. MY FAULT:
LIFE'S ULTIMATE SIN.
(1069)

HOW DO I APPEAR?
IS THERE CAUSE FOR CHEER, OR CRING-
ING IN FEAR OF MIRTH?
(1058)

I HAD A GOOD THING:
BLEW IT. KNEW IT WASN'T RIGHT.
DID IT JUST FOR SPITE.
(1056)

LIKE MOST, I DON'T DARE
LOOK AT LIFE TOO CLOSELY: SCARED
OF WHAT I WOULD SEE.
(1053)

I'M NOT LIKE YOU – OR
THE REST. IF YOU'RE THE BEST THEY
CAN DO – NO CONTEST!
(1047)

I'M OUT OF RAGE. I
BURNT IT ALL. THAT UNLOCKED MY
CAGE. NOW, I FREE-FALL.
(1046)

I TRY. I FAIL. I
WHINE. I WAIL. OPENING'S FINE –
JUST CAN'T CLOSE THE SALE.
(1033)

I LIKE PAIN. IT'S MY
OUT: LET'S ME SUSTAIN MY CLAIM
I'M NEVER TO BLAME.
(1032)

APOSTATE, I WREAK
UNMITIGATED HAVOC THAT
WILL NEVER ABATE.
(1021)

I PRETEND TO BE
DEBONAIR, AN *"I DON'T CARE"*
TYPE – PAIN SPARING HYPE!
(1013)

I'M WHO I HAVE TO
BE. AREN'T YOU? IF THIS OFFENDS,
WHO GIVES A DAMN? SCRAM!
(990)

THERE'S A TERRIBLE
SORROW SHROUDING MY SOUL: NO
FRIENDS, ALONE – MY TOLL.
(986)

I KNOW, ALL TOO WELL,
THE VALLEY OF WOE. IT'S WHERE
I DWELL – IN SHADOW.
(979)

MOODY, MANIC, MIRED
IN CONTRADICTION, I AM
STRANGER THAN FICTION.
(974)

SARCASM REQUIRES WIT,
INTELLECT AND HUMILI-
TY. FEW HAVE A CLUE.
(973)

DOUR CYNICISM'S
BLEAK, BLACK NIGHT CLOAKS ADVO-
CATE'S ANGER AND FRIGHT.
(969)

I'M RARELY WHO I
OUGHT TO BE 'CAUSE I'M BARELY
WHO I THOUGHT I'D BE.
(966)

CURSED AS A CHILD BY
RECTITUDE; NOW AGED, BLESSED
WITH A WILD ATTITUDE.
(963)

MY DAILY FARE, BLEAK
DESPAIR, GRIMLY FILLS THE BLACK
HOLE THAT IS MY HEART.
(958)

ALL I SEE AROUND
IS NEED AND GREED. PRAY TELL,
HOW CAN WE PROCEED?
(957)

HAVING ABANDONED
HOPE, UNABLE TO COPE, I'M
ON A SHORT, THIN ROPE.
(956)

I SAVOR EACH WIN
WITH AN INTERNAL GRIN. THEY'RE
RARE. ONLY I CARE.
(955)

INTENSE, EMOTION-
AL, RIGHT BRAINED, ARTSY: EASY
TO CAST DARTS AT ME.
(951)

BEHIND ME IN A
CAR? HEED! THE CLOSER YOU ARE
THE SLOWER I ARE.
(950)

AS I CONTEMPLATE
MY WINTER YEARS, ONE GREAT FEAR
HAUNTS ME – RELEVANCE.
(931)

FEARFUL OF TAINTING
THEIR SOUL, MANY WORSHIP THAT
FALSE IDOL CONTROL.
(926)

I DO WHAT I HAVE
TO. THE THING IS: I'M NOT
SURE WHY I HAVE TO.
(923)

EGO'S DELUSIONS
CAUSE GREAT PAIN AND CONFUSION.
GET OVER YOURSELF!
(921)

A KIND WORD HERE, A
SMILE THERE, DO WONDERS TO SHOW
SOME OF US DO CARE.
(910)

MY LIFE NOW ISN'T ME.
SOMETIME, SOMEHOW, I LOST TOUCH.
WHO AM I? WHO'S ME?
(909)

GOT IT. I KINDA
THOUGHT WE WERE ON THE SAME PAGE.
GUESS I READ TOO FAST.
(902)

WISE WORDS THESE: OTHERS'
LIES MAY WOUND; ONES WE TELL OUR-
SELVES BE TRAGEDIES.
(893)

MEMORY'S OBLI-
GATIONS, BITTER SWEET, OFT FORCE
ONE'S NEEDS TO RETREAT.
(890)

WHAT CAME BEFORE IS
SUCH A BORE! WE'RE HERE SO THE FUSS
OUGHT TO BE ABOUT US.
(887)

TRUTH BE TOLD (NOT OF-
TEN) AS FOLKS GROW OLD, THEY TEND
TO SCOLD, NOT SOFTEN.
(886)

O.K. I ADMIT
I DON'T FIT IN -- A MISFIT
WHO DOESN'T EVER WIN.
(881)

I'VE LOVED, WITH NO RE-
TURNS. MY HEART SCREAMS *"WHY?"* AND, WHILE
I CRY, MY SOUL YEARNS.
(877)

WE THINK REASON DIC-
TATES CHOICES. NO WAY! MOSTLY,
OUR HEART HAS THAT SAY.
(876)

MORE OF A CLOWN THAN
A BUFFOON, I'LL GET IT TURNED
'ROUND – AND NONE TOO SOON!
(874)

I'M NOT GOOD FOR ME.
I SEE WHAT I WANT, IGNOR-
ING REALITY.
(869)

NICE I'VE SELDOM BEEN –
MUCH TO MY CHAGRIN. LEARN FROM
ME – OR HAVE NO FRIEND.
(867)

NIGHT'S MY FRIEND. DARK HIDES
MUCH. DAY'S MY ENEMY. THINGS
I SEE DISRUPT ME.
(865)

FACT: CAVORTING WITH
CONTORTIONISTS PUTS ONE
IN AWKWARD POSITIONS.
(857)

AVOID THIS ALLEY:
TOO MUCH ME; RARELY WE; I;
OR, YOU'LL BE LONELY.
(835)

MY REASONING'S PRE-
CARIOUS, WHIM TO GRIM, NE-
FARIOUS HAUNTINGS.
(813)

MOST MINDS DISLIKE DE-
TOURS. MINE CRAVES ROUND ABOUTS AND
OFF-ROAD ADVENTURES.
(806)

I'M NOT LIKE ANY
OF YOU. MY WIRING'S ASKEW.
WHAT TO DO? NO CLUE.
(800)

HAPPINESS, FRAGILE,
COMES AND GOES, SCARRING US WITH
MANIC HIGHS AND LOWS.
(750)

WHEN YOU'RE IN THE GAME
YOU'RE NOT SURE WHO TO BLAME. ON
THE WAY OUT, NO DOUBT!
(743)

PERCEPTIONS GIVE RISE
TO EXPECTATIONS WHICH THEN
COLOR NEW PERCEPTIONS.
(736)

DROWNING. SINKING BE-
NEATH MY TEARS. TRYING TO FOR-
GET ALL OUR WASTED YEARS.
(735)

RISABLE, LACHRY-
MOSE, I REMAIN INVISI-
BLE. NO ONE GETS CLOSE.
(732)

OTHERS LOOK, EVEN
STARE. THEY CAN'T TELL. NOTHING SHOWS.
BUT I SEE. I KNOW.
(731)

WANTING TO AVOID
PAIN, WE CLOSE OURSELVES OFF FROM
FEELING. WHO'S HURT MOST?
(720)

BOOKISH; SARCASTIC;
NO FRIEND OF SMALL TALK, MY DI-
RECTNESS OFFENDS MOST.
(719)

HAD A FEW CHANCES
IN LIFE. BLEW'EM. THOUGHT I COULD
DO BETTER. SO DUMB.
(713)

IT'S TIME. NO MORE PUT-
TING ON MY GAME FACE. FROM NOW
ON, IT'S AGE WITH GRACE.
(703)

I HAVE TO PUT SOME
MILES 'TWEEN ME'N THEE. IF I DON'T,
I'LL NEVER BE FREE.
(702)

I LIED. SO DID YOU.
LIFE'S TOUGH: ALL PLAYERS LIVE TO
SEE WHO CALLS WHO'S BLUFF.
(699)

MY GREATEST FEAR ISN'T
DYING. IT'S DYING ALONE,
UNLOVED, WITH NO ONE.
(695)

UNDER NO MAN'S SWAY,
I'LL HAVE MY OWN SAY. COME WHAT
MAY, I CHOOSE MY WAY.
(693)

NO JUDGE OF MOTIVES,
STUBBORNLY NAÏVE, I TRUST
WHILE BEING DECEIVED.
(687)

MY DELUSION'S THAT
I'M IN CONTROL OF MY LIFE.
AT ALL TIMES. WHAT'S YOURS?
(679)

I'M NOT SURE WHO I
AM AND SCARED OF WHAT I MIGHT
BECOME OR, WORSE, DO.
(634)

WALLOWING IN SELF-
PITY JUSTIFIES MY DE-
LUSIONS OF GRANDEUR.
(628)

LOOKING BACK, THERE'S ONE
THING I'D DO DIFFERENTLY –
ALL AFTER AGE FOUR.
(601)

I'LL BE GREATLY SUR-
PRISED IF ANYONE SHOWS UP
FOR MY FUNERAL.
(600)

CHASING RAINBOWS, IG-
NORING LIFE'S SMALL BLESSINGS, HAS
ITS PRICE: I'M ALONE.
(598)

CREATIVITY'S
BRIGHT FLAME FEEDS ON ITSELF 'TIL,
SPUTTERING, IT'S OUT.
(596)

PERCEPTIVE, BUT NOT
INTUITIVE, TOO LATE I
SEE WHAT I SHOULD'VE FELT.
(594)

I'M DEPRESSED, DISTRESSED
AND OBSESSED OVER YOU. GUESS
I SHOULD REASSESS.
(592)

THE ESSENCE OF CO-
OPERATION IS YOU DO-
ING WHAT I TELL YOU.
(591)

I AM THE MOST DE-
SPISED PERSON IN TOWN. OBEYING
SPEED LIMITS DOES THAT.
(575)

A FAÇADE OF IN-
DIFFERENCE PROVIDES THE SHROUD
FOR MY LOSS OF HOPE.
(549)

A CULTURED SECRET
SNOB, I HIDE BEHIND A RED
NOSE OF CLOWNISH WIT.
(532)

MOST OF US SAY AND
DO THINGS IMPULSIVELY. SOME
WE CAN FIX. SOME NOT.
(527)

TRUE CHARACTER TEST:
OBSERVE DRIVING ETIQUETTE,
IT'S EYE OPENING.
(525)

WE ALL NEED TO KNOW
THIS: HOW LOW WILL I GO? WHAT'S
MY ROCK BOTTOM LINE?
(507)

I MAY HAVE RUN OUT
OF THINGS TO SAY, BUT TOMOR-
ROW'S ANOTHER DAY.
(493)

I LOVED YOU. I LOST
YOU. IT HURTS. NOT ALL BAD, THOUGH:
I KNOW WHAT LOVE IS.
(461)

I AM WHAT I AM.
IT'S NEVER TOO LATE TO CHANGE
SO, I MIGHT ... OR NOT.
(459)

LAMENTING FRIENDSHIPS
NOT MADE, CONNECTIONS BROKEN,
I WILL MAKE AMENDS.
(441)

WISDOM SUGGESTS MOD-
ERATION IN ALL THINGS. GUESS
I BETTER WISE UP.
(439)

WITTY, WISE, I AL-
WAYS HAVE THE PERFECT RETORT --
TEN MINUTES TOO LATE.
(412)

I FUME. I RAGE. I
SPIT INVECTIVE. REASON'S FOOL,
ANGER CONSUMES ME.
(406)

OVERTHINKING BRINGS
HESITATION, WHICH IS PER-
CEIVED AS ALOOFNESS.
(392)

SHY, NO MASTER OF
REPARTEE, I'M RESIGNED TO
ANONIMITY.
(388)

IT'S NOT ALWAYS OB-
VIOUS THAT WHEN HELPING SOME-
ONE, WE HELP OURSELVES.
(375)

I'VE LIVED MY LIFE LIKE
I DON'T CARE. I DO. ALWAYS
HAVE. SAD NO ONE KNOWS.
(369)

ONE MUST FIRST ADMIT,
AND ACCEPT, THEIR IGNORANCE
IN ORDER TO LEARN.
(368)

MOST OF US HAVE HAD
THIS: FOOT-IN-MOUTH DISEASE CAUSED
BY *"TALK-FAST, THINK-SLOW."*
(367)

DISCONNECTED, MY
MELANCOLY AND ALOOF-
NESS WIDEN THE GAP.
(349)

LACKING SOCIAL GRACE,
WE WRETCHED CAROM THROUGH LIFE,
DISGUSTING THOSE THUS BLESSED.
(326)

IN MY LONELINESS
HOPE MINGLES WITH DELUSIONS
TO RAVAGE MY PRIDE.
(311)

I DON'T HAVE MUCH CHARM;
PLENTY OF WIT, HUMOR TOO.
FUNNY CAN BE SWEET.
(310)

THOSE FEELINGS FROM A
JOB WELL-DONE ARE THEIR OWN RE-
WARDS. YOU TREATING YOU.
(305)

HERE'S HOW I COPE: I
EXPECT THE WORST, ALL THE WHILE
NEVER LOSING HOPE.
(301)

I DO WHAT I CAN,
WHEN I CAN. I DON'T DO WHAT
I CAN'T. SIMPLE.
(294)

IN THE DEPTH'S OF MAN'S
SOUL DWELLS A DEMON WAITING
TO DEVOUR US ALL.
(291)

EGO INFLATES WITH
POWER GAINED. ALWAYS HAS BEEN
SO – 'TIL MAN'S NO MORE.
(283)

CHOOSE WORDS CAREFULLY.
MANY ROUSE STRONG EMOTIONS.
KNOW YOUR AUDIENCE.
(271)

I'M NOT LOVED. MY FAULT.
TOO LATE I YEARN FOR LOVE, TO
SHARE WITH ANOTHER.
(256)

THE PRICE OF BEING
A CONTROL FREAK IS TOTAL
LACK OF COMPASSION.
(229)

A LIFETIME'S REGRET
CAN RESULT FROM A MOMENT
OF ANGER UNLEASHED.
(224)

WHAT WE THINK WE'RE WORTH
AND HOW OTHERS VALUE US –
OUR TRUTHS VERSUS THEIRS.
(222)

IF I SAY TO YOU
"YOU SHOULD BEHAVE AS I DO!"
PLEASE! PUNCH OUT MY LIGHTS.
(213)

PERFECTION'S PURSUIT
BRINGS ONE SORROWS, FRUSTRATION
AND LIFETIME MALAIS.
(203)

GIVING YOUR KIDS TOO
MUCH MIGHT GET OUT OF HAND – MAKE
THEM FEEL ENTITLED.
(202)

QUERY (YOU HAVE TO
GET THIS RIGHT!): IF THINGS GO SOUTH
WHO YOU GONNA TRUST?
(201)

THE OUTSIDE'S ALL SHOW,
WHAT WE WANT OTHERS TO SEE.
INSIDE'S WHAT MATTERS.
(199)

IF YOU DON'T KNOW WHAT
YOU'VE LOST WHEN YOU LOSE IT, HOW
YOU GONNA FIND IT?
(198)

WE ALL POSSESS THAT
INNER VOICE WHIS'PRING "THAT'S WRONG!"
VERY FEW LISTEN.
(196)

IGNORANCE BREEDS AN
ARROGANCE PECULIAR TO
FEAR GRIPPED, IDLE MINDS.
(195)

NOTE TO FUTURE SELF:
TRY TO BE MORE ACCEPTING
OF ALL THINGS HUMAN.
(192)

FEELING SORRY FOR
YOURSELF, POOR THING? WHO'S TO BLAME?
QUICK! FIND A MIRROR.
(179)

GET ANGRY EASY?
TAKE A DEEP BREATH; COUNT TO TEN;
THINK BEFORE SPEAKING.
(177)

DOES LIFE HAVE PURPOSE?
IF YES, WE SHOULD *ALL* SHARE IT.
IF NO, WHAT THE F@#%?
(174)

WE'RE DEFINED BY OUR
PERSONAL INTEGRITY.
IT MAKES – OR – BREAKS US.
(161)

FEAR FREEZES US IN
PLACE OR SPARKS US TO ACTION.
USE IT – FREE YOURSELF.
(160)

HALF FULL? HALF EMPTY?
HOW WE SOLVE THIS CONUNDRUM
SHAPES OUR PATH THRU LIFE.
(156)

I WAS NEVER ONE
TO CONNECT WITH OTHERS: JUST
OUTSIDE, LOOKING IN.
(155)

CHANGE IS A GIVEN.
ADAPT OR GET LEFT BEHIND.
NO OTHER OPTIONS.
(153)

I KNOW I LOVE YOU.
NOT SURE THE REVERSE IS TRUE.
WHAT TO DO? HOPE'S FOOL!
(152)

DON'T BE THINKIN' YOU
GOT PLENTY OF TIME. NOT SO –
TIME *ALWAYS* RUNS OUT.
(151)

NOTHING'S BLACK OR WHITE.
NUANCED, SUBTLE HUES OF GRAY
COLOR OUR CHOICES.
(149)

PERSPECTIVES VARY.
EACH OF US HAS A UNIQUE
WORLD VIEW. WHAT CHANCE PEACE?
(148)

WOULD I WERE A POE,
SHELLEY OR GIBRAN. THEN I
MIGHT DO YOU JUSTICE.
(131)

WHAT'S MOST IMPORTANT –
WHAT OTHER'S THINK; WHAT THEY SEE;
OR WHAT YOU KNOW'S TRUE?
(125)

ANGER SHROUDS ONE'S SOUL
IN A MIND-NUMBING BLACKNESS
THAT OBSCURES ALL LIGHT.
(121)

AS THE YEARS COLLECT,
CYNICISMS VILE CLAWS CLUTCH
MY SOUL, STRANGLING IT.
(84)

THERE ARE THOSE OF US
WHO DON'T PLAY WELL WITH OTHERS.
"FATHER FORGIVE THEM ..."
(76)

BE KIND TO YOURSELF.
WE'RE ALL OUR OWN WORST CRITIC.
HELL! LIFE'S TOUGH ENOUGH.
(52)

MONEY CAN'T BUY IT.
NOT EVEN LOVE IS ENOUGH.
SELF-ESTEEM IS ON YOU!
(50)

OF ALL HUMAN TRAITS
COMPASSION'S MOST NEEDED AND,
SADLY, MOST LACKING.
(48)

THERE'S WHAT WE SAY, DO,
THINK, HEAR. BUT, ... IN WHICH LANGUAGE?
WHEN? WHERE? WHAT IS TRUTH?
(39)

LIKE IT OR NOT, HERE'S
A REAL NO-BRAINER: WE'RE
ALL IN THIS TOGETHER!
(36)

QUICK QUIZ! WHO AM I?
LET'S SEE: WHAT AM I WILLING
TO RISK IT ALL ON?
(35)

THAT KISS ... OUR EMBRACE;
TIME'S RAVAGES, DO YOUR WORST;
OH, I'LL REMEMBER!
(31)

BOOK FIVE

SOCIAL COMMENTARY

THE DELUSION OF
CERTAINTY LEADS MANY TO
ACT DISPICABLY.
(2100)

HAVING IT ALL – WOW!
WHAT A BALL! – JUST SETS YOU UP
FOR A HARDER FALL.
(2096)

SEEING SHOULDN'T BE
BELIEVING. BRAINS LIE – WHAT EYES
RECEIVE IS DECEIVING.
(2095)

HUMANITY'S IN-
CREASING INSANITY: D
M'D FROM HIGH TECH'S CLOUD?
(2094)

THE WHY OF IT IS
THE LIE OF IT: GREED AND/OR
EGO IN A SNIT.
(2093)

THINGS MEN DO ARE FEW:
SEX, MONEY, POWER. NONE NEW,
MERELY NEWLY DONE.
(2092)

KNOWING WHO YOU NEED
TO BE, THEN MAKING THAT BE
TRUE. HAPPENS RARELY.
(2091)

MAN'S HISTORY IS
GUARANTEE THAT FEW, IF AN-
Y, ARE TRULY FREE.
(2086)

THESE WORDS: *"I'M FREE. I'LL
DO AS I PLEASE"* BRING SOCI-
TIES TO THEIR KNEES.
(2082)

GREED. DUPLICITY.
TWIN THREADS WEAVE MANKIND'S HISTO-
RY, SPINNING DECEIT.
(2080)

YES! I DON'T /WON'T DO
SOCIAL MEDIA. THAT MAKES
ME TABOO TO YOU!
(2072)

TIME'S TAUGHT ME TO SEE
LIFE'S REALITY AS VAUDE-
VILLE ABSURDITY.
(2069)

GENDER/RACE HATE HIDE
IN EGO'S NEED TO DOMI-
NATE AND POWER'S GREED.
(2067)

FEW GRASP POWER'S EVIL
TWIN, CORRUPTION, EVEN
WHEN IT DOES THEM IN.
(2058)

TOO MUCH FREEDOM BRINGS
"ME! ME!" TOO LITTLE DEVOLVES
INTO TYRANNY.
(2050)

DATA FLOWS AT HIGH
RATE. BRAINS CAN'T COLLATE, OVER-
LOAD. TEMPERS EXPLODE.
(2031)

LACKING EMPATHY,
MANY DWELL IN HELL'S OPI-
UM DEN *"ME!, ME!, ME!"*
(2019)

HIGH TECH'S THE PREACHER
AT MANKIND'S WAKE: ALL BLESSINGS
TO/FOR THE CLOUD'S SAKE!
(2018)

THESE DAYS ANY FEEL-
ING PERSON MUST BE REELING
IN SHOCK AND DISGUST.
(2017)

VALUES ARE TRIBAL
WITH LOCAL PROTOCOLS, ET
AL: *"DIVIDED WE FALL!"*
(2012)

BRETHREN! MEND THY WAYS.
ATTEND TO THINE OWN FAULTS, NOT
SEEKING OTHERS' PRAISE.
(1992)

AN IMPRECISENESS
OF INTELLECT CAUSES YOUR
REAL-TIME DISCONNECT.
(1981)

SHY, IGNORANCE HID
AWAY. THE INTERNET NOW
LETS IT OUT TO PLAY.
(1979)

A CALL TO BE WILD
IS RECONCILED IN OUR MINDS
BY OUR INNER CHILD.
(1978)

IF I DO WHAT I
SAY, CHEER ME. UNTIL THAT DAY --
JUST STAY CLEAR OF ME!
(1951)

WE EACH PERCEIVE FAIR
UNIQUELY. BASICALLY
IT'S: *"WHAT WORKS FOR ME."*
(1920)

HOW DO WE DEFINE
TRUTH, WHEN WE CAN'T AGREE ON
WHAT IT IS? BEATS ME.
(1919)

HOW CAN THIS BE? ALL
THREE MAJOR RELIGIONS SEE
THEIR CREED AS *"GOD'S WILL."*
(1918)

MY TRUTH DENIES YOURS.
WHAT'S THE CURE? EASY.WE GRAB
SOME GUNS, HAVE SOME FUN.
(1916)

412

PURPORTING TO BE
BEST FOR ME, RELIGION TESTS
MY AUTONOMY.
(1911)

COMPROMISE MEANS AC-
CEPTANCE AND TOLERANCE. MOURN
IT'S DISSAPEARANCE
(1910)

FOR A MAJORI-
TY, FREE MEANS *ME ONLY, NOT
YOU*" – LIKE THREE YEAR OLDS.
(1908)

SELF-RIGHTEOUS, INCRED-
ULOUS, WE NEGATE SHARED TRUTHS
THAT SHOULD UNITE US.
(1907)

WHEN IS THERE NOT A
CONFLICT SOMEWHERE? MAN IS AN
ADDICT TO WARFARE.
(1898)

REALITY'S SHROUD
IS THE FANTASY FORMING
THE INTERNET CLOUD.
(1887)

A CULT OF *'ME'* HAS
MELTED THE GLUE – TOLERANCE – OF
MAN'S SOCIETY.
(1885)

THERE'S LITTLE EVI-
DENCE THAT INTELLIGENCE HAS
RELEVANCE THESE DAYS.
(1865)

FOR FREE! HERE'S A BREAK-
DOWN OF SOCIETY'S COM-
PLEXITY: *'ME FIRST!'*
(1850)

YOU FEW WITH PLENTY
VIEW THE DESTITUTE MANY
AS AN ENEMY.
(1849)

JUSTICE ISN'T BLIND. LOOK
CLOSELY. YOU'LL FIND SHE SEES WHAT
BIG MONEY SEES ... SEE?
(1848)

GUMPTION AND GALL ARE
ALL ONE NEEDS TO SUCCEED IN
SOCIETY'S GAMES.
(1843)

BRED IN DUPLICI-
TY, FED BY COMPLICITY,
POLS SHOUT OUT *WHO ME?"*
(1839)

TO SPREAD BLAME TWEET, TEXT
OR FACETIME ANOTHER'S NAME:
OUR TIME'S *"NOT ME"* GAME.
(1832)

INTERNET'S BEAUTY:
THERE'S ABSOLUTELY NO RE-
SPONSIBILITY.
(1822)

ENEMIES OF DI-
VERSITY CONDEMN MAN TO
MEDIOCRITY.
(1797)

OLD: POVERTY. NEW:
(P.C.) IMMUNITY FROM
OPPORTUNITY.
(1790)

A FEW WAGGING TONGUES
HERE … WHISPERING IN AN EAR …
STRANGE RUMORS APPEAR.
(1787)

NOT HARD TO SEE WHAT
AILS SOCIETY: TOO MUCH
'ME', TOO LITTLE *'WE'*.
(1732)

REMEMBER *'SIMPLE'*?
THOUGHT NOT. WE WORSHIP AT OUR
TIME'S NEW TEMPLE – BLING.
(1731)

FLIPPANT AND SARCAS-
TIC ARE RELEVANT RETORTS
TO BOMBASTIC RANT.
(1711)

HIGH TECH'S IN-
FECTED SOCIETY: FEELINGS, REASON
GONE TO ELECTRONS.
(1709)

WHEN WE'RE ALL *"FREE"*, WHAT
THEN? NATURES PRIME LAW KICKS IN:
EAT! OR BE EATEN.
(1706)

SOCIALLY ACKWARD?
A BRUTISH LOUT? DON'T WORRY:
MONEY SORTS THAT OUT.
(1704)

VILE BLACK GUARDS WE BE,
WHO WANTONLY SEEK TO PROF-
IT FROM MISERY.
(1702)

MOST PRETEND TO MAKE
AMENDS. SEETHEING INSIDE, THEY
BIDE THEIR TIME. HATE HIDES.
(1616)

THE RARITY OF
INNATE CHARITY'S EASY
TO SEE: *"ME! ME!"*
(1601)

SO MANY ELECTRONS
HAVE BEEN RE-ROUTED THAT *"TRUTH"* CAN'T
BE RECONSTITUTED.
(1596)

SOME FIND IT AMUS-
IN' TO SPREAD CHAOS AND CON-
FUSION. THEN THEY WIN.
(1565)

GAMING: MAN'S SUPREME
GOAL. WIN AT ALL COSTS, REGARD-
LESS WHAT'S GAINED – OR LOST.
(1560)

IF I THINK IT'S TRUE,
IT MUST BE. WHEN YOU CAN'T SEE,
TOO, MORE'S THE PITY.
(1559)

SEEKING INCLUSION
IS AN ILLUSION, FED BY
SOCIAL DELUSION.
(1558)

THE ESSENCE OF VAN-
ITY AND DIRGE OF SOCI-
ETY IS: *"ME!" "ME!"*
(1546)

WE SELF-DECEIVE 'TIL
WE BELIEVE, THEN DON'T GRIEVE FOR
OUR INIQUITY.
(1534)

WE'VE BECOME WHAT WAS
FEARED: LIVE ROBOTS WHOSE ACTIONS
APPEAR ENGINEERED.
(1532)

WHEN IS *"FAIR"* FAIR? FEW
SHARE ITS MEANING, SAVE *"IF I
WIN, THEN ALL IS FAIR."*
(1528)

MOST CHOOSE VIOLENCE
AND WAR OVER PEACE. WHAT'S OUR
FUTURE HAVE IN STORE?
(1482)

OF ALL THOSE GAMES WE
PLAY, WITH THEIR DIRTY TRICKS, THE
WORST IS POLITICS.
(1443)

GREED'S DIRECTLY PRO-
PORTIONAL TO THE ABSENCE
OF NEED. MORE CRAVES MORE.
(1405)

MORE AND MORE EACH DAY
FEWER ALLOW FACTS AND TRUTH
TO GET IN THEIR WAY.
(1403)

SPITTING IN THE WIND'S
FUN FOR MASOCHISTS; SOUL-LIFT-
ING FOR DADAISTS.
(1394)

SUBJECTIVITY
DISTORTS OBJECTIVITY.
NEVER FAIR. FEW CARE.
(1393)

SHE DIED TODAY. NO
ONE NOTICED OR CRIED – JUST STEPPED
ASIDE, ON THEIR WAY.
(1392)

ETHICS TAKES A POW-
DER AS THE CRESCENDO OF
"ME!" "ME!" ROARS LOUDER.
(1391)

SEARCH YOUR MIND. RECALL
A TIME WHEN WE THOUGHT ALL WERE
KIND AND LIFE SUBLIME?
(1390)

STREET LIVES. UNSEEN. CAUGHT
BETWEEN DO-GOODS AND THE RIGHT:
HIDDEN IN PLAIN SIGHT.
(1389)

TRUST PASSED TODAY. SHE
FOUGHT, BUT GREED AND SELF-INTER-
EST SPED HER DECAY.
(1382)

EQUALITY'S A
RING-MASTER'S DREAM – BARNUM, P.
T.'S SUCKER-PUNCH SCHEME.
(1381)

ONCE IN THE CLOUD YOU'RE
STUCK THERE. YOU CAN'T ESCAPE AN-
YWHERE. BEST BEWARE.
(1377)

THOSE THAT ARE LITER-
AL ARE, RARELY, LIBERAL.
GRAY MAKES THEIR NERVES FRAY.
(1372)

WHEN WE DON'T AGREE
IN A DEMOCRACY WE
INVITE ANARCHY.
(1340)

SOCIETY ISN'T
FREE. WE AGREE TO LIVE IN
FIXED BOUNDARIES – LAWS.
(1338)

LOOKS LIKE WE'VE CHOSEN
"FREEDOM" OVER UNITY.
WHAT'S NEXT? PLEASE! TELL ME.
(1322)

HUMAN NATURE HAS
ALWAYS BEEN "ME." "ME." STUDY
HISTORY. YOU'LL SEE.
(1317)

MY FIST IS THE ONE
SOCIAL MEDIA CHANNEL
THAT CAN'T LIE TO YOU.
(1299)

WHEN IT'S ALL FALSE NEWS,
NOTHING'S TRUE. WE CAN ALL DO
WHAT WE WANT TO. YEAH!!
(1274)

WE SHOULD HAVE A PLACE
WE GO, WHEN WE CAN'T FACE WHAT
WE DON'T WANT TO KNOW.
(1271)

WHICH HAS THE STRONGER
SPIN: (A) TYPHOON; (B) POLI-
TICIAN? LIES, GRINS WIN.
(1265)

THOSE FAST YEARS WE'RE HERE
JUST DISAPPEAR. FEW ADJUST
ERE BECOMING DUST.
(1264)

ROME FELL. SPAIN – SAME. SO ...
USA? CAN'T RIGHTLY TELL.
THINGS AIN'T GOIN' WELL.
(1263)

A LAMENT: INTENT,
NOT ACCOMPLISHMENT, IS WHAT'S
MEANT BY *"RELEVANT."*
(1261)

IT'S OBVIOUS: THERE'S
NO HUMAN PROGRESS UNLESS
IT'S FOR ALL OF US.
(1260)

MOST CHOOSE TO CONFUSE
THEIR LIVES WITH LIES, THEN ALI-
BIS. DON'T ASK THEM WHY!
(1255)

SAY WE ALL GET OUR
WAY. HOW'D THAT BE? ... HELL WOULD BE
VIEWED AS COMEDY.
(1233)

THEY WHO INVOKE *"FREE-
DOMS"* OFT NEGLECT OUR SOCIAL
CONTRACT ENABLING THEM.
(1226)

WE WANT TO BELIEVE
"WE'RE IN THIS TOGETHER." – AIN'T
HARD TO SELF-DECEIVE.
(1217)

THOUGH YOUR TELLING'S QUITE
COMPELLING, I'M JUST NOT BUY-
ING WHAT YOU'RE SELLING.
(1117)

LIKE LIKES LIKE. THEY DON'T
ACCEPT DIFFERENT, ONLY
THOSE IN AGREEMENT.
(1035)

FOR MANY THE COST-
TO-VALUE MARGIN OF FEEL-
INGS ISN'T WORTH THE RISK.
(1030)

THE WORDS MOST OFTEN
HEARD? *"I." "MY." "ME."* ENOUGH SAID!
SOCIETY'S DEAD.
(981)

WRIT LARGE, THAT WRITING
ON THE WALL WARNS ALL. YET … MOST
MINDS REMAIN *"ON CALL."*
(960)

TECH, DATA OBSESSED,
IS CANCER TO MAN'S EMPA-
THY AND COMPASSION.
(949)

TIME, SPACE, DAYS, MONTHS, YEARS
DON'T SET A PACE FOR US. WE'RE
A RACE OF THE SPHERES.
(942)

IN THE ABSTRACT, PEACE
MUST HOLD SWAY. WAIT! THAT
REQUIRES COMPROMISE. NO WAY!
(941)

THE PATH TO PARA-
DISE LIES NOT THROUGH RIGHT OR TRUTH:
ONLY COMPROMISE.
(937)

MORALTITY'S IN
THE CLOUD; EHTHICS'RE AT GUANTAN-
AMO; GAME-SET-MATCH.
(936)

SOCIETY UN-
RAVELS AT THE PACE HIGH SPEED
INTERNET TRAVELS.
(929)

THE ONLY PEOPLE
I'M SCARED OF ARE THOSE WHO KNOW
WHAT'S BEST FOR US ALL.
(920)

DISCUSSIONS BETWEEN
LEFT AND RIGHT SHOULD BE: DO WHAT'S
RIGHT OR NOTHING'S LEFT.
(916)

SHOW ME A POLI-
TICIAN WHO'S NOT A HIPO-
CRITE. 'TWAS NEVER WRIT!
(879)

WHEN EGOS CLASH NO-
ONE WINS. PUT TO THE TEST, MOST
WILL FIND CHINS OF GLASS.
(849)

AS I PERUSE WHAT'S
FOISTED AS NEWS, I'M DIFFUSED BY
A DESIRE TO SNOOZE.
(841)

IN MY HAY DAY -- YEARS
AGO – I HAD LOTS TO SAY.
NOW? I KNOW BETTER.
(832)

FUN'S BEGUN! "LOOSE THE
DOGS OF WAR." WHEN THIS ONE'S DONE
WE WILL BE NO MORE.
(812)

THE ADVENT OF "DE-
VICES" IS MAN'S MOST DEVIS-
IVE SOCIAL EVENT.
(810)

FROM CAVEMAN TIME'S THERE'S
BEEN VIOLENCE. EXCEPT FOR
TOYS, NOTHING'S CHANGED SINCE.
(763)

"I'M SORRY." TODAY'S
"F!@K-OFF!" ISN'T SINCERE: IT'S MEANT
TO SAVE FACE. "SORRY."
(757)

BEAUTY: STRIVING FOR
PERFECTION KNOWING IT CAN'T –
EVER – BE ATTAINED.
(756)

MOST DISTAIN PASSION.
IT'S INTENSIITY DISRUPTS
THEIR FRAGILE SELF-WORTH.
(755)

THERE AREN'T MANY LEFT
WHO BELIEVE IN "ONE NATION,
INDIVISIBLE. "
(727)

MOST CAN'T GET PAST THEIR
BELIEFS. WORSE – THEY TRY TO FORCE
THEM ON ALL OF US.
(724)

MOST OF THE GOOD STUFF
IN LIFE IS HIDDEN IN PLAIN
SIGHT. OPEN YOUR MIND!
(718)

SOCIETY'S SOUL –
THE CONCEPT OF 'WE' - IS CLOUDED
BY HIGH-TECH'S "ME! ME!"
(717)

INCESSANT CONTEN-
TIOUSNESS AND *'WIN-AT-ALL-COSTS'*
MINDSETS PRESAGE DOOM.
(681)

MOST THINK SAYING *"I'M
SORRY"* RIDS THEM OF THE BLAME
FOR CAUSING PROBLEMS.
(651)

EGO-CENTRIC, NAÏVE,
CRAVING ATTENTION, MANY
'POST' THEIR LIVES FOR 'LIKES.'
(626)

FACTS ARE NO LONGER
RELEVANT TO TRUTHS: JUST USE
YOUR *"FACTS"* FOR YOUR *"TRUTHS."*
(589)

RESTRAINT AND MANNERS
GET LOST IN THE CLOUDS OF OUR
SELFIES-TWEETS-LIKES WORLD.
(588)

INVARIABLY,
IDEOLOGY INTRO-
DUCES INVECTIVE.
(556)

PROFESSIONAL POL-
ITICIANS PERPETUATE
PANDEMONIUM.
(555)

MENDACIOUS, MALI-
CIOUS MALCONTENTS MANIPU-
LATE MEN'S MEMORIES.
(539)

CYNICAL CONGRESS-
MEN CREATE CHRONIC CONSTI-
TUTIONAL CHAOS.
(538)

PRIMEVAL, PREDA-
TORY PREDILECTIONS PER-
MEATE POLITICS.
(537)

NO FANATIC'S FIT
COMPANY FOR ANY SAVE
FELLOW DEVIANTS.
(521)

SELF-DECEPTION'S ON-
LY LIMITS ARE THE DECEIVEDS'
ACCEPTANCE OF TRUTHS.
(519)

GAMES WITHIN GAMES. DE-
CEITS WITHIN DECEPTIONS. HU-
MANS AT PLAY. WHAT FUN!
(466)

IT APPEARS YOU SLEPT
THROUGH BASIC SCIENCE: EARTH OR-
BITS THE SUN, NOT YOU.
(464)

IF WE IGNORE THE
MIDDLE PATH, DON'T COMPROMISE,
WE'LL ALL GO STRAIGHT ... DOWN.
(462)

IF YOU GET HURT CALL
A LIMOSINE. IT'S CHEAPER
THAN AN AMBULANCE.
(460)

GOD FORBID WE'RE ALL
HAPPY AND CONTENT! HOW COULD
WE EVER PROGRESS?
(457)

FOR MANY, LOOKS DO
COUNT. PLEASE EXPLAIN WHY! WHAT DOES
THIS SAY ABOUT US?
(456)

THE PRETEXT OF SE-
CURITY LENDS TYRANTS RA-
TIONALE FOR MAYHEM.
(435)

IN AN EMERGEN-
CY, WHATEVER YOU DO, DON'T
CALL YOUR CONGRESSMAN!
(433)

LOCKS AND LAWS ARE FOR
HONEST PEOPLE. HOW MANY
DO YOU THINK YOU KNOW?
(431)

SPOILED CHILDREN, ALSO
MOBSTERS, BEHAVE BETTER THAN
MOST POLITICIANS.
(420)

THE SPECTACLE THAT'S
TODAY'S POLITICS PUT P.
T., BARNUM TO SHAME.
(378)

BLACK, WHITE, RED, YELLOW,
BROWN. HUMAN SKIN HUES. OUR ON-
LY DIFFERENCES.
(377)

THE GAME PLAYED BY MOST
CANDIDATES? GIVE'EM HOPES, BUT
VERY FEW RESULTS.
(339)

WE USED TO BE THE
FAMILY OF MAN. NOW, WE'RE
SAVAGES AMOK.
(299)

FAIR OR FOUL? IS THIS
A CONCERN? DOESN'T MATTER
ONLY WINNING COUNTS.
(290)

HEARD THIS ONE? – SEEMS A
PLANET GAVE LIFE TO CREATURES
WHO THEN DESTROYED IT.
(289)

HIGHER LEARNING'S GOAL
OUGHT TO BE: TEACH THEM TO THINK,
NOT JUST GET A JOB.
(277)

BEING TOO WORDY
TENDS TO CONFUSE AND DISTRACT.
USE FEWER. BE HEARD.
(270)

SKIN TONE, GENDER AREN'T
DISQUALIFIERS IN OUR
SHARED HUMANITY.
(262)

A PRECIOUS FEW DO
SO MUCH FOR THE REST OF US.
KEEP THEM IN YOUR HEARTS.
(254)

FACEBOOK; YOUTUBE; ALL
SOCIAL MEDIA SCREAMS: *"I*
LIVE IN A FISHBOWL!"
(253)

OUR HUMANITY'S
DAILY COMPOSTED INTO
HIGH TECH'S DATA CLOUDS.
(242)

ANGER MANAGEMENT
ISSUES GROW APACE WITH HIGH
TECH'S INCREASING SPEEDS.
(236)

THINK EARTH'S NOT WARMING
UP? CHECK THE OCEAN LEVELS.
HOPE WE GROW GILLS, FAST!
(235)

OLD MEN START WARS FOR
PROFIT AND POWER. YOUNG MEN
THEN FIGHT FOR "GLORY."
(223)

THE BIRDS AND BEES ARE
PREFERRED OUTLETS TO MISSLES,
GUNS, BOMBS AND ARMIES.
(211)

UNDERSTATEMENT'S GONE.
TODAY, IT'S MOD, GAUDY, CHIC-
IN YOUR FACE. TRÈS GAUCHE.
(191)

IT'S LATE, CLOCK'S TICKING.
NOT MANY OPTIONS REMAIN.
PLANET'S BURNING UP.
(187)

WELL, ONE THING'S CERTAIN:
WE WILL NEVER STOP KILLING
ONE ANOTHER. WEEP!
(186)

FAR FROM UNITING
US, RELIGIONS SEPARATE
US INTO ARMED CAMPS.
(185)

MORAL DECAY AND
SOCIAL ROT – TWIN SIBLINGS OF
PRESENT DAY "PROGRESS."
(182)

THERE ARE THOSE OF US
FOR WHOM BEAUTY IS LIKE BREATH:
ITS ABSENCE MEANS DEATH.
(176)

FOR SOME, A LITTLE
IS A LOT. FOR OTHERS, A
LOT IS TOO LITTLE.
(175)

HIGH TECH'S DETRIMENTS
OUTWEIGH ITS BENEFITS. WE
KNOW MORE, LISTEN LESS.
(174)

NO ONE WINS IN WAR.
EVEN THE "WINNERS" LOSE. THINK
WE WILL EVER LEARN?
(173)

NO USE ASKING WHY.
TRUTH'S RELATIVE – OR A LIE.
WHAT IS, IS. THAT'S ALL.
(112)

POLITICIANS LIE.
SOME BOLDLY. OTHERS SUBTLY.
GO WITH THE SMOOTHEST.
(111)

VIETNAM DID ME
IN. PRIOR: I TRUSTED ALWAYS.
SINCE: CYNICAL WRETCH.
(92)

NO MATTER HOW LOW
YOU THINK MOST POLITICIANS
WILL GO, YOU'RE TOO HIGH!
(70)

WOW! HOW TIMES HAVE CHANGED!
THESE DAYS SLEAZY AND RUDE TRUMP
REFINED AND POLITE.
(67)

CONTEMPT RESULTS WHEN
ARROGANCE OF BIRTH OR MIND
EXALTS ONE'S STATUS.
(66)

POSTERIOR VERSE

IF THIS BE FOLLY
LOOSE YOUR VOLLEY. WOULD YE PRAISE,
WHY, LET VOICE BE RAISED!
(2112)

Made in the USA
Monee, IL
30 June 2022